JEAN VANIER

MODERN SPIRITUAL MASTERS
Robert Ellsberg, Series Editor

Already published:

Dietrich Bonhoeffer (edited by Robert Coles)
Simone Weil (edited by Eric O. Springsted)
Henri Nouwen (edited by Robert A. Jonas)
Pierre Teilhard de Chardin (edited by Ursula King)
Anthony de Mello (edited by William Dych, S.J.)
Charles de Foucauld (edited by Robert Ellsberg)
Oscar Romero (by Marie Dennis, Rennie Golden,
    and Scott Wright)
Eberhard Arnold (edited by Johann Christoph Arnold)
Thomas Merton (edited by Christine M. Bochen)
Thich Nhat Hanh (edited by Robert Ellsberg)
Rufus Jones (edited by Kerry Walters)
Mother Teresa (edited by Jean Maalouf)
Edith Stein (edited by John Sullivan, O.C.D.)
John Main (edited by Laurence Freeman)
Mohandas Gandhi (edited by John Dear)
Mother Maria Skobtsova (introduction by Jim Forest)
Evelyn Underhill (edited by Emilie Griffin)
St. Thérèse of Lisieux (edited by Mary Frohlich)
Flannery O'Connor (edited by Robert Ellsberg)
Clarence Jordan (edited by Joyce Hollyday)
G. K. Chesterton (edited by William Griffin)
Alfred Delp, S.J. (introduction by Thomas Merton)
Bede Griffiths (edited by Thomas Matus)
Karl Rahner (edited by Philip Endean)
Sadhu Sundar Singh (edited by Charles E. Moore)
Pedro Arrupe (edited by Kevin F. Burke, S.J.)
Romano Guardini (edited by Robert A. Krieg)
Albert Schweitzer (edited by James Brabazon)
Caryll Houselander (edited by Wendy M. Wright)
Brother Roger of Taizé (edited by Marcello Fidanzio)
Dorothee Soelle (edited by Dianne L. Oliver)
Leo Tolstoy (edited by Charles E. Moore)
Howard Thurman (edited by Luther E. Smith, Jr.)
Swami Abhishiktananda (edited by Shirley du Boulay)
Pope John XXIII (edited by Jean Maalouf)
The Dalai Lama (edited by Thomas A. Forsthoefel)

MODERN SPIRITUAL MASTERS SERIES

JEAN VANIER

Essential Writings

Selected with an Introduction by
CAROLYN WHITNEY-BROWN

ORBIS BOOKS

Maryknoll, New York 10545

Founded in 1970, Orbis Books endeavors to publish works that enlighten the mind, nourish the spirit, and challenge the conscience. The publishing arm of the Maryknoll Fathers and Brothers, Orbis seeks to explore the global dimensions of the Christian faith and mission, to invite dialogue with diverse cultures and religious traditions, and to serve the cause of reconciliation and peace. The books published reflect the views of their authors and do not represent the official position of the Maryknoll Society. To learn more about Maryknoll and Orbis Books, please visit our website at www.maryknoll.org.

Library of Congress Cataloging-in-Publication Data
Vanier, Jean, 1928-
    [Selections. 2008]
    Jean Vanier : essential writings / selected with an introduction
by Carolyn Whitney-Brown.
        p.   cm. – (Modern spiritual masters series)
    ISBN 978-1-57075-806-5
    1. Christian life – Catholic authors.   2. L'Arche (Association)
I. Whitney-Brown, Carolyn.   II. Title.
BX2350.3.V38 2008
248.4 – dc22
                                                    2008019687

We have discovered how important it is
to celebrate birthdays in L'Arche,
to help people recognize and re-read their personal histories....
Birthday celebrations provide a chance to
emphasize certain stages in their lives,
highlight their gifts,
laugh about their faults or failures,
and celebrate each one's unique gifts.
— Jean Vanier, *An Ark for the Poor*

This book is mostly by Jean Vanier, but it is also for Jean Vanier,
to help celebrate his first eighty years.
It is dedicated to his mother and father, his sister and brothers,
the members of L'Arche and of Faith and Light,
and all the thousands of people who have touched his life
and made him who he is.

Happy birthday, Jean!

Contents

Sources

ARK   *An Ark for the Poor: The Story of L'Arche* (Toronto: Novalis, 1995; London: Geoffrey Chapman, 1995).

BH   *Becoming Human* (Toronto: House of Anansi, 1999; Mahway, N.J.: Paulist Press, 1999; London: Darton, Longman & Todd, 1999).

BNA   *Be Not Afraid* (Mahwah, N.J.: Paulist Press, 1975; Toronto: Griffin House, 1975; Dublin: Gill and Macmillan, 1975).

BSL   *Be Still and Listen* (Richmond Hill, Ont.: Daybreak, 1975).

BTS   *Befriending the Stranger* (Toronto: Novalis, 2005; Grand Rapids, Mich.: Eerdmans, 2005; London: Darton, Longman & Todd, 2005).

CG   *Community and Growth*, rev. ed. (London: Darton, Longman & Todd, 1989; New York: Paulist Press, 1991).

CLA   *The Challenge of L'Arche* (London: Darton, Longman & Todd, 1982; Ottawa, Ont.: Novalis; Minneapolis: Winston Press, 1981). Introduction and conclusion by Jean Vanier.

DMJ   *Drawn into the Mystery of Jesus through the Gospel of John* (Toronto: Novalis, 2004; London: Darton Longman & Todd, 2004; New York: Paulist Press, 2004).

EH   *Eruption to Hope* (Toronto: Griffin House, 1971; New York: Paulist Press, 1971).

Introduction

Change the world, with love, one heart at a time.

Two events on August 4–5, 1964, offer contrasting choices. A report was circulated of a North Vietnamese attack on American destroyers in the Gulf of Tonkin on August 4, 1964. The U.S. president addressed the nation and retaliated on August 5, bombing North Vietnam. In the ensuing ten years, more than two million Vietnamese and fifty-eight thousand American soldiers were killed. The original Gulf of Tonkin incident was later revealed to be a complete fabrication.

At the same time, across an ocean in France, an extraordinary community was beginning quietly. On August 4, a thirty-six-year-old Canadian former naval officer named Jean Vanier moved into a dilapidated house. On August 5, he was joined by Raphaël Simi and Philippe Seux, two men with intellectual disabilities who had been living in an institution. It was the first L'Arche community. In the following decades, more than 132 L'Arche communities have begun in over thirty-four countries, welcoming people of all faiths and traditions. Its related network of Faith and Light has more than fifteen hundred communities, and Jean Vanier has become internationally known for his profound reflections on social inclusion, peace, forgiveness, and what it means to be human.

Over and over, Vanier emphasizes the great discovery of his life: "that we are healed by the poor and the weak, that we are transformed by them if we enter into relationship with them, that the weak and the vulnerable have a gift to give to our world. They call us together, in unity and peace, to build community." Jean's parallel conviction is that the poor and weak are also ourselves, each one of us. Living in this reality is a cornerstone of peace.

In a world of pain and violence, of cynicism and manipulation, of walls between people and countries, L'Arche was begun as a small sign of hope, concrete proof that a community of peace is possible.

Vanier's influence has been recognized in major national and international awards. His insights have been gained through more than forty years of living in his own L'Arche community and extensive travels around the globe.

A committed Roman Catholic, Vanier has created his identity outside of conventional Catholic church roles, outside of ecclesiastical structure. He is a lay person, celibate, committed to his community and to avoiding, when possible, the waste and luxury of his culture. Vanier left his early career as a military officer feeling his call in life was elsewhere. He is not easily categorized, a spiritual leader who is not a priest, a philosopher and Ph.D. who is not a professor.

My first introduction to Vanier's writings was through a small piece of what he calls "meditative prose." It was the mid-1970s, and my friends and I were struggling to understand how to live well in the world. We analyzed economic theories, political movements, and alternative cultural experiments. We read the Gospels. In every way, we were idealistic, earnest, young, beset by a constant, vague guilt about our culture and the North American way of life.

I remember the day a friend sent me a letter with a quotation from Jean Vanier:

> But if I get too near this woman
> if I listen to her
> if I begin to know the names of her children
>> her past
>> her life
>> If I identify with her

> I can't go on eating as I used to
> I can't accept the luxury and the waste
>
> If I truly love
> if I feel concerned
> my life must change
>
> the time I get up and go to bed
> the friends I like to talk with
>   go out with
>   eat with in smart restaurants
>
> the books I read
> the money I have to spend ... (*BNA,* 17)

It was a short meditation, but I read it over and over until I had memorized it. Nothing I had read before had spoken to and for my heart, my deeper longings, in this way.

As I look back, three things about this reading grabbed me. First, Vanier was trying to dig deeper into understanding the roots of his own fear. I knew I was uneasy around people who seemed to ask too much of me, but I hadn't thought to ask myself exactly what I feared. Vanier was gently and directly exposing how personally threatening our choices could be to our comfortable lives.

Second, I saw in a new way the conflict between my desire for greater fairness and justice in the world, and my life stretching ahead, which I wanted to be familiar and pleasant. "Luxury and waste" were part of my culture, in part beyond my individual choices. Vanier was not offering answers, but was helping me name the reality of my inner and outer cultural ambivalence.

And finally, Vanier was identifying relationships as the way into the world that my friends and I simultaneously longed for and feared.

Nearly twenty years later, as my husband and I were finishing Ph.D.'s at Brown University, we decided to change directions and learn more about prayer and community. While doing doctoral research in England, we had visited a L'Arche house called Bethany in Bognor Regis for several days. We were fascinated by its lively chaos, so different than the rare book libraries where we spent our time. On our last evening, one of the men read about Martha and Mary and Lazarus from a book of Gospel stories by Jean Vanier. "Jesus loves them very much," he read slowly. "He often goes to their home to rest." We could see why Jesus would like to rest in L'Arche. We decided to explore possibilities beyond academic careers.

After two years of living with several intentional communities in the U.K. and Africa, we moved to L'Arche Daybreak in Canada, the community in which Henri Nouwen was also living. We were members of L'Arche Daybreak from 1990 to 1997. Our three children were born in those years.

When Jean Vanier visited the community, we would celebrate his visit with songs, skits, and community discussions. Vanier would fold his tall frame into a chair and take in our offerings, his face alight with fun. I remember one visit, when he was about to address the community in the afternoon. David Harmon, long-term member of Daybreak, dragged a mat to the front and sprawled out at Vanier's feet. "You always put me to sleep, Jean," he commented.

Vanier smiled delightedly and addressed us all. "This is that dangerously sleepy time after lunch. It's all right if you go to sleep. I'll keep talking as long as one person is still awake." Then he leaned forward and spoke quite earnestly. "But when you wake up, listen. That is the prophetic word for you, the word for which you've been awakened."

Vanier's life choices have been based on his conviction that for each of us there are prophetic moments that God will initiate, the wake-up calls of our lives. Every person, no matter how socially marginalized, has a unique call and purpose from God in the world.

Family and Childhood

Vanier's life spans a critical period of change, from his coming-of-age during World War II to the environmental, globalized issues of the early twenty-first century. He was born in Switzerland on September 10, 1928, to Canadian parents. At the time, his father was military advisor to the Canadian delegation to the League of Nations in Geneva. Vanier was born into a family impressive for its commitment to public service and its deep faith.

Jean Vanier's maternal grandmother's ancestors had come to North America in the 1730s. His grandmother, Thérèse de Salaberry Archer, was a deeply spiritual woman, whose gentle spiritual director also guided St. Thérèse of Lisieux. His maternal grandfather had been named to the Superior Court of Quebec at the young age of forty-two. They had one child, Pauline. When World War I erupted, she applied to be a foot soldier. Turned down, she turned her courage and generosity to train as a nurse. She worked long hours in a military convalescent hospital until the end of the war. By 1919, Pauline Archer had applied to a convent. But then she met Georges Philias Vanier in Montreal over tea at the Ritz-Carlton.

Georges Vanier was a young Montreal lawyer when World War I began in 1914. Accounts from Europe awakened his compassion and desire to right the wrong he saw. He helped to organize Canada's first French-Canadian volunteer unit, the Royal 22nd Regiment, now famous as the "Van Doos." Wounded in battle, his right leg amputated, he returned to Canada a respected and decorated officer, and met Pauline. They found in each other a partner in spirit, in love for God, in courage and service. They were married in 1921.

Jean Vanier was the fourth of the five Vanier children. His father and mother were by then already known and loved in diplomatic circles. Vanier grew up, as he describes it, "in a deeply religious Catholic family. My parents, even with all their busyness and social position, shared a deep faith and spent half an hour each day together in silent prayer."

He left for England, and did not live with his parents again. It marked the end of what most people consider their childhood. It was also an early sign of the many intuitive choices that would shape his adult life.

Vanier's Career in the Navy, 1942–50

Vanier crossed the Atlantic safely and went to his sister's home in London. There was no way to tell her exactly when he would arrive, so she came home one evening to find "this pathetic little form sound asleep on the doorstep with all his belongings scattered around him." Vanier, looking back, notices how his adolescent years in the navy formed his body and strength, pushing him to focus his energies and idealism. "I had an adolescence which was completely geared without wavering to one thing," he notes, "and that thing was not at all materialistic."

Vanier's education at Dartmouth offered academic subjects, sporting activities, as well as seamanship and sailing. He was among the better students of his class, and also played tennis and rugby. When the college was bombed just before Vanier's second term began, students were moved to an alternative location. The Vanier family had many friends in England. The daughter of one family recalls fourteen-year-old Jean Vanier coming for holidays. "He was very dashing in his naval uniform, delightful, unusual, full of energy. He was not shy, but quite at ease with himself. He taught me an American pop song!"

One of few Roman Catholics at the college, Vanier recalls the curious practice of ordering Catholics to "fall out" during formal parade. The Catholics would step forward, turn smartly, go behind a hedge, and say the "Hail Mary" while the other students said the prayer all Christians share, "Our Father." It was his first experience of awkward ecumenical accommodation.

When Paris was liberated in August 1944, Georges Vanier, Canada's ambassador to France, was the first accredited diplo-

mat to arrive in the city. Pauline Vanier went with him. Jean
Vanier recalls:

> A few months after the liberation of Paris, I accompa-
> nied my mother, who was in the Canadian Red Cross, to
> the Gare d'Orsay in Paris — the train station where hun-
> dreds of men and women arrived like skeletons in their
> striped blue and white uniforms, from Dachau, Buchen-
> wald, Ravensbrook, and other concentration camps. (Un-
> published talk)

He still recalls vividly the people, "their faces tortured with
fear, anguish, and pain." The horror of the Hiroshima bomb
and the instantaneous deaths of tens of thousand of people also
affected him deeply. "We became very conscious of the capacity
of humanity to destroy itself." As a young person, Vanier was
directly confronted with many aspects of both the technology
and the human cost of war.

By January 1946, Vanier had completed his training and
began life on the sea. Over the next eight months, he traveled to both the West Indian and Scandinavian coasts. In 1947
Vanier was appointed to the H.M.S. *Vanguard,* which took
King George VI and the royal family to visit South Africa.
On board, there were teas and deck games with the royal
princesses, Elizabeth and Margaret, who were about the same
age as the young officers. He recalls some of the gifts and
limitations of those years:

> Like the French and Canadian navies, the British navy is a
> powerful institution in which there is a great sense of be-
> longing. We were proud to be in the navy and we loved
> the whole way of life in warships. There was a bond of
> real friendship between the officers. The uniform, the tra-
> ditions, and the naval trappings created a strong *esprit de
> corps.* Personal life, meanwhile, was kept to a minimum.
> The way of life strengthened in all of us a spirit of courage,
> hard work, loyalty, honesty, and co-operation. (*OJH*, 175)

Further studies in science, literature, and sublieutenant's training in gunnery, submarines, communication, combined operations, and other subjects followed. "I could wield weapons, and I could help direct ships of war," Vanier notes. Moved around England for these courses, Vanier made an effort to attend Mass wherever he was appointed. His conscious faith began to awaken and grow.

Vanier transferred to the Canadian Navy, and was based in Halifax as an officer on the *Magnificent*, Canada's only aircraft carrier. He found a spiritual director, read his breviary, and attended Mass daily.

Vanier was twenty-one in the spring of 1950, when the *Magnificent* went to Cuba on exercises with the U.S. Navy. While his brother officers went out dancing, he became aware that his interests were elsewhere: he was more interested in finding a church. He was reading the American monk Thomas Merton's autobiography, *The Seven Storey Mountain*, and seized a stop in New York to go to Harlem to visit Friendship House. Delighted with that community of people who were marginalized and poor, he ended up spending all his free time in New York with his new friends. This connected with his growing desire to follow Jesus and the Gospel message in a deeper way. Before his ship left port, he invited fifteen people from Friendship House to dinner in the officers' dining room on board the *Magnificent*.

As Vanier matured through his experiences, reading, and reflection, he became conscious of a desire to change his life direction.

> When I was in the navy, I was taught to give orders to others. That came quite naturally to me! All my life I had been taught to climb the ladder, to seek promotion, to compete, to be the best, to win prizes. That is what society teaches us. In doing so, we lose community and communion. (*FBC*, 18)

Vanier's metaphorical use of the "ladder" has a curious irony. Sometime in 1947, Vanier had nearly died falling off a rope ladder in gusting winds and rough seas. He lost consciousness immediately and was swept away by the strong current, held up by his life jacket. Remarkably, the boat's chaplain and some sailors who had spotted his fall were able to catch up with him in a small boat and pull him to safety. "It was perhaps the only experience I have had of coming close to death," Vanier ponders. "I believe it was a small miracle of Providence that I was saved."

By 1950, Vanier chose to fall off the ladder of promotion into the arms of Providence. Just as his intuition had led him into the navy eight years before, now Vanier's heart and spirit were yearning to live the Gospel call in a different way. After a thirty-day retreat following the Spiritual Exercises of St. Ignatius, Vanier had made his decision. He resigned his position in the navy, with little future direction other than a hunger to follow Jesus and live according to the Gospels.

Studies, Solitude, and Searching, 1950–64

"My place in the world was somewhere else," Vanier felt, but there was no clear model for the kind of search to which Vanier felt called. Unlike the navy, which as soon as it accepted him took full responsibility for his education and formation, Vanier would now need to follow his intuition.

Pauline Vanier introduced her son to her spiritual director, a Dominican priest named Thomas Philippe. The powerful bond that was immediately formed with "Père Thomas" would shape the rest of his life.

Père Thomas's story is an interesting one in itself. Born in 1905, one of twelve children, he was certain of his vocation to the priesthood by the time he was five years old. At twenty-four he was ordained as a Dominican, and since 1942 had been a professor, first in Rome then at the Saulchoir near Paris.

In 1947, he began Eau Vive, a small community close to the Saulchoir for students to study philosophy and theology while living a communal life of love, reconciliation, and charity. It was not a wealthy establishment. Simple accommodations and food made it possible for students with very little money to join. It was the first place of study in France to welcome a German student after the war. A friend who came to visit Vanier there in 1951 described "Arabic philosophers, a Persian merchant, several Germans, a woman who went into a concentration camp for being a key worker in the 'underground' during the war." The eighty students came from twenty countries, with a strong Middle Eastern contingent. Visiting professors such as Jacques Maritain, Charles Journet, and Oliver Lacombe (a scholar of Hindu mystical experience) taught summer courses.

Père Thomas hoped Pauline Vanier could help him fundraise for the community. Pauline Vanier was less taken with the proposed fundraising role than with the Dominican's strong intuitive sense of her inner spiritual journey.

Looking back, Jean Vanier emphasizes that, though he was not searching consciously for a place of nourishment or development, he found it. Most deeply, Vanier says, he was looking for "a place to be born." Like his mother, Vanier had a powerful experience of spiritual connection with Père Thomas. He counts "two great moments" in his life: his father's trust when he was thirteen, and meeting Père Thomas, which he experienced as "true liberating love." In a 2005 interview, he notes that Père Thomas didn't give answers: he provided tools for people to be able to recognize and understand the choices in their lives. Père Thomas would listen and then say, "Pray about it." He didn't tell Vanier what to do, but "helped me to discover the Holy Spirit within me. His was a pedagogy of helping people to trust themselves to trust God." Vanier threw himself into his studies, the manual work of the community, and direction, both intellectual and spiritual, from Père Thomas.

In April 1952, Père Thomas was removed by Rome for unorthodoxy and for spiritual direction that was considered too mystical. It was the period in which Rome also removed worker priests, as well as ordained professors who seemed too caught up in psychology, communism, or other contemporary intellectual movements. Vanier was asked by the board to assume the leadership of Eau Vive, and he stayed until 1956. Students were no longer able to study at the Dominican Saulchoir, but instead at the Institut Catholique in Paris. Numbers in the community dwindled, though summer courses continued.

Vanier could have been ordained a priest and had made inquiries about the process. At one point, it seemed he would be ordained in Quebec and sent back to Eau Vive as chaplain. His mother happily purchased a stole and chalice in anticipation. But as he discerned his call, including a 1959 visit with his parents to their old friend, now Pope John XXIII, Vanier became aware that his path was elsewhere. He needed the freedom to respond to God's Spirit by following his own intuition. Trusting himself as his father had trusted him in his teens, trusting the Holy Spirit within him as Père Thomas had encouraged him, he became convinced that he needed to listen for his call from God outside the ecclesiastical structure.

After leaving Eau Vive, Vanier continued to work on a doctorate through the Institut Catholique, studying Aristotle's understanding of happiness. Vanier identifies his fascination with Aristotle, whose fundamental orientation both resembled and shaped Vanier's own:

Aristotle is one of the great witnesses to this quest for happiness. His thinking was not that of an ideologue, but based on human facts and personal experience. That was what led him to propound his ethics of happiness in order to help people to look more clearly into themselves and to find their own fulfillment. He did so twenty-four hundred years ago, but his thinking spans the centuries and is still relevant to us today....

Aristotle does not, however, seek merely to reiterate moral axioms. Nor does he wish to prompt people by external means to be just, to seek the truth, and to obey laws. What he wants to do is lay the foundations of a moral science with thinking that stems from humanity's deep desires. His fundamental question is not "What ought we to do?" but "What do we really want?" His ethics are not those of law. Rather, they look closely at humanity's deepest inclinations in order to bring them to their ultimate fulfillment. Aristotle's ethics are not therefore based on an idea but on the desire for fullness of life inscribed in every human being. (*MH*, x–xi)

Vanier worked on his doctoral thesis from the Trappist monastery of Bellfontaine, then in greater solitude in small cottages, first in Orne, then in Fatima. Longing to follow Jesus and to live simply, Vanier focused on his studies, times of prayer, and daily Mass.

In June 1962, Vanier defended his thesis, "Happiness as Principle and End of Aristotelian Ethics," and was graduated as a Doctor of Philosophy *cum maxima laude*. His thesis went deeper than an intellectual exercise. It provided intellectual foundations for the intuitive choices that continued to shape his journey:

My research into the basis of Aristotelian ethics brought me a great deal of light and helped me to grasp the connection between ethics, psychology, and spirituality. Psychology helps us to understand human behavior and grasp the fears and blockages that are in us, in order to help us free ourselves of them. Spirituality is like a breath of inspiration that strengthens our motivation. Ethics help us to clarify what is a truly human act, what justice is and what the best activities are — those that render us more human and happiest. They help us better understand to what our freedom is calling us....

Many of Aristotle's principles are valid for any ethics. Being human does not mean simply obeying laws that come from outside, but attaining maturity. Being human means becoming as perfectly accomplished as possible. If we do not become fully accomplished, something is lost to the whole of humanity. For Aristotle this accomplishment derives from the exercise of the most perfect activity: that of seeking the truth in all things, shunning lies and illusion, acting in accordance with justice, transcending oneself to act for the good of others in society. (*MH,* xiii–xv)

He was offered a temporary teaching position at St. Michael's College, University of Toronto, starting in January 1964.

Just before Christmas 1963, Vanier and other friends of Père Thomas helped Père Thomas move into two modest rooms in Trosly, France, and refurbish one as a chapel. Père Thomas had accepted a position as chaplain to the Val Fleuri, a small institution for men with intellectual handicaps. Père Thomas quickly found affinity with both the rejected and marginalized population of the Val Fleuri and with the poor villagers of Trosly. As Père Thomas described it: "After many different services and hardships of all kinds, God led me to Trosly to be with people with an intellectual disability; those who are poor in their head, in their person, but who have such a love for Jesus."

Vanier's visit included a theatrical production at the Val Fleuri. The experience touched him, but he was self-conscious among the men there, not immediately at ease. This was a reasonable response, both to the noise, commotion, and violence of the Val, and to people unlike any he had previously spent time with. Still, Père Thomas offered Vanier the idea that he might do "something" with people with intellectual disabilities.

Through that winter at St. Michael's in Toronto, Vanier rapidly became a popular teacher. Although it was his first teaching experience, he had an aptitude for shaping the material to interest students. Hired to teach ethics, he began with

questions of justice, but found his students "weren't terribly interested" in those ethical questions. Vanier adjusted his themes
to explore ethics through the meaning of friendship and sexuality. Drawn by Vanier's charisma and insights, students filled
and overflowed his classes.

Vanier was offered a permanent position at St. Michael's College, but he wanted to be close to Père Thomas and all that
Père Thomas was learning. As soon as the term was over, he
went back to France. "Père Thomas and I had the deep conviction that we had been called together by Jesus to accomplish
something," Vanier wrote later.

1964 and the Early Years of L'Arche

Despite his own discomfort, Vanier had been impressed by the
men who were becoming Père Thomas's friends. He pondered
what he had seen: so much life, suffering, and longing for
friendship. "Their cry of pain and their thirst for love touched
me deeply." Père Thomas's suggestion that maybe Vanier could
do "something" had stayed like a planted seed through the
teaching term.

In France, Vanier visited centers for people with intellectual
disabilities. He was struck by people's screams and the heavy
atmosphere, yet also by a mysterious presence of God. "I was
touched by these men with mental handicaps, by their sadness,
and by their cry to be respected, valued, and loved." A similar
hunger was growing in Vanier, who had never considered the
human weakness or longings in himself.

> Since I was a child, there have been three very distinct
> stages in my life. When I was thirteen, I joined the navy
> and spent eight years in a world where weakness was
> something to be shunned at all costs. We were required
> to be efficient and quick and to climb up the ladder of
> success. I left this world, and another world opened up

to me — the world of thought. For many years, I stud-
ied philosophy. I wrote a doctoral thesis on Aristotelian
ethics, and I embarked on a teaching career. Once again,
I found myself in a world where weakness, ignorance,
and incompetence were things to be shunned — efficiency
was everything. Then, during a third phase, I discovered
people who were weak, people with mental handicaps. I
was moved by the vast world of poverty, weakness, and
fragility that I encountered in hospitals, institutions, and
asylums for people with mental handicaps. I moved from
the world of theories and ideas about human beings in
order to discover what it really meant to be human, to be
a man or a woman. (*OJH*, 33)

The "something" Père Thomas had suggested was taking shape
in Vanier's mind: a small "foyer" or family-sized house to share
with some of the men he had met in his visits to institutions.

Vanier consulted his parents, who were now back in Canada.
In 1959, Georges Vanier had been appointed Canadian Gover-
nor General, Canada's highest office, a position he held until
his death in 1967. Georges and Pauline Vanier were now well-
known public figures, enormously beloved throughout Canada.
Pauline Vanier was not taken with her son's latest idea. Their
trusted friend Tony Walsh encouraged them to support Jean's
vision, seeing in it a Gospel inspiration in the same spirit as his
own Benedict Labre House in Montreal, which offered accommodation and friendship to homeless men. Deciding yet again
to trust the intuitions of their unconventional son, Vanier's parents helped Vanier buy a small house in Trosly-Breuil, within
walking distance of Père Thomas.

"Practically everything I did with L'Arche was intuitive,
based on the sense that this is what should be done," Vanier
recalls. Pieces rapidly fell into place. Friends helped with practical aspects, such as the legal structure that would link it with
an already established charitable foundation. Vanier had known
American Jesuit Dan Berrigan in New York years before. Now

over a meal in Paris, Vanier shared his plans, and Berrigan introduced him to Louis Pretty, a Canadian architect. Pretty helped Vanier design and furnish his house and was an essential part of the founding of L'Arche, before returning to a distinguished career in Canada.

With the help of the directress of an asylum for the intellectually handicapped that Vanier had visited, he chose three men. His invitation was for a one-month holiday, and at the end of the month, the possibility of a permanent home would be confirmed. Looking back, Vanier sees that, for him, this invitation was simply the right thing to do, with a sense of urgency to follow the signs of the Spirit.

On August 4, 1964, Vanier moved into "L'Arche," a house so simple that there was no toilet, only a bucket, and no electricity. On August 5, he was joined by Raphaël Simi, Philippe Seux, and a third man named Dany. A celebratory welcome luncheon officially launched the new community. Then the guests departed, and the four men were left together.

The first night, Dany was so needy and disturbed that Vanier recognized a small house could not meet his needs. The next day Vanier regretfully returned him to the familiar routines of his institutional life. The other two men endured the primitive comforts, disciplined structure of the day, and playful celebration that Vanier offered, gradually teaching Vanier deep truths about building authentic community. Vanier knew, too, that with these two men, Raphaël Simi and Philippe Seux, he had made an irrevocable choice for his life. This was the beginning of L'Arche: a vision, a desire, an audacious risk, an immediate wrenching failure and new wisdom gained even that first night.

"There is a time for all things," Vanier reflected, echoing Ecclesiastes. There was a time to join the navy, and a time to leave it. There had been a time for spiritual and intellectual formation. In 1964 there was a time for Vanier to make a commitment to people, to assume responsibilities, to put down roots. He knew "there was no turning back."

It turned out the house had electricity. A few days later, Vanier located the electric meter, which helped enormously. Poverty attracted friends. The little house was full of laughter as well as struggles. Vanier did all of the cooking, except when neighbors brought food. Vanier and Seux and Simi began to know each other. "Our prayer was magnificent," Vanier remembers. His first circular letter was dated August 22, 1964, and gratefully acknowledged the generosity of many friends. L'Arche had begun.

Vanier does not like to think of himself as "the founder," explaining: "At the beginning of it all there was a call from God, a call revealed to me through Père Thomas. L'Arche was not my project, it was God's" (*LL*, 2).

In a way, it is a story with a curiously mythic and familiar shape. The son of a distinguished family with high ideals of service joins the military in wartime. Reading the Gospels awakens a different kind of idealism for spiritual service. Living simply, often in solitude, he broadens his horizons through studies and also gets to know people who are very poor. Moved by these real relationships, recognizing his own poverty, he forms a community to live simply with the poor. Drawn by his vision and charisma, others come to join him. Soon communities exist on three continents, and continue to grow.

Vanier's life does follow the pattern of many faithful Christians, such as St. Francis, St. Ignatius, St. Martin. But each life is unique and part of its particular historic moment. Vanier was not alone. Simi's and Seux's choice to join and stay with Vanier showed enormous courage and trust.

Vanier adds, "I feel also that L'Arche and Faith and Light have grown because of contemplatives who are holding us in prayer," such as Sr. Marie Madeleine, a Carmelite, the Carmelites in Cognac, and many others. The deep and constant commitment to prayer of many friends was an unseen but crucial contribution that has also shaped and sustained L'Arche.

> During those first months, I learned a great deal. I was be-
> ginning to discover the immense amount of pain hidden
> in the hearts of Raphaël, Philippe, and so many of their
> brothers and sisters. I sensed how much their hearts had
> been broken by rejection, abandonment, and lack of re-
> spect. At the same time, I was beginning to discover some
> of the beauty and tenderness of their hearts, their capacity
> for communion and tenderness. I was beginning to sense
> how living with them could transform me, not through
> awakening and developing my qualities of leadership and
> intelligence, but by awakening the qualities of the heart,
> the child within me. (*LL, 3*)

The little house hummed along for several months, its circle of
friends and support expanding rapidly. Then came an enormous
change.

At the end of 1964, all the staff at the Val Fleuri resigned ef-
fective in March. Vanier was asked to become director of this
institution where thirty-two men with various intellectual disabilities lived and worked. Vanier, happy in his new L'Arche
home, was reluctant to add such enormous responsibility so
soon. This new challenge did not arise from his own intuitive
urging. However, after discussions, Vanier agreed that it seemed
to be the next step. Père Thomas, still chaplain at the Val, felt
it was what Jesus wanted.

In March 1965, Vanier moved to the Val Fleuri. Two staff
members remained to help. The previous director offered min-
imal information, handed him a large, heavy bundle of keys to
files, offices, and cupboards, and left. Within an hour, the keys
were stolen and were never recovered. Vanier remembers, "I felt
very alone."

The Val, with its constant noise, shouting, and frequent violence, was very different than the small L'Arche house. "L'Arche
was no longer a small prophetic community where we were living poorly with the poor. There was a budget to draw up and
an accounts sheet to balance," Vanier recalled.

Vanier accepted the challenge with good energy. He learned the names of all thirty-two men rapidly and opened the gates of the institution. He practiced giving injections on an orange to be able to administer medication to a diabetic resident. The Val Fleuri had to meet state norms and be accountable to local and national government officials. Vanier quickly began to cooperate with professionals, learning about employment requirements and salaries. Again, the poverty of the situation attracted friends. Volunteers came from the village to help with gardening, bookkeeping, and cooking.

By November 1965, Vanier was writing his circular letter with news of "our two communities," the Val Fleuri and L'Arche. "May I ask if any of you have any old bird cages or bicycles?" he inquires. "Those of us who are most disabled could care for and watch the birds; others, accompanied by an assistant, could take bike rides in the forest."

The L'Arche communities also traveled together on holidays and pilgrimages. In 1966, community members made a pilgrimage to Rome and were received by His Holiness Pope Paul VI for an audience on Wednesday in Holy Week. "Seeing you all together makes us realize that you are a small group united by love and an active will to help one another. You are a community in whose midst Jesus is happy to live," declared the pope. "God calls all of you, in spite of your difficulties, to be saints, and He reserves a special role for you in His Church.... We count on you, dear Sons, and we bless you."

Vanier recalls those trips as "opportunities for fun and adventure." His life had given him an enthusiasm for traveling, and Vanier considers journeys and celebrations important in three ways. They keep up people's spirits, open hearts to new realities, and break up routines of everyday life in order to meet new people and face unexpected challenges. The communities found the activity of pilgrimage to a holy place deepened their bonds with each other, healed divisions, and created new connections. These trips deepened and reinforced what L'Arche was trying to live.

L'Arche was growing. For years, Vanier returned each year to St. Michael's in Toronto and other universities to lecture, and to visit family and friends. These were also times of connecting beyond the community in Trosly. At a 1965 conference in Montreal with William Stringfellow, Vanier became friends with an Anglican couple, Steve and Ann Newroth, and a Jesuit priest named Bill Clarke. Both would come to L'Arche soon afterward. The lectures also led to other invitations, such as an invitation, unusual at the time, for a layperson to lead a retreat for priests:

> I was asked to give a retreat to the priests in the diocese of Toronto. This invitation took me by surprise. I felt incapable of giving an immediate answer. I needed time to pray and reflect. Finally, it seemed quite clear that Jesus wanted me to answer "Yes" but under three conditions: that it be a silent retreat; that it last eight days; and that it be open not only to priests but also to vowed religious and to lay people. The retreat took place in August 1968, in Marylake near Toronto. I was naïve (as always) and petrified, yet at the same time trusting in Jesus. I had entrusted this retreat to the prayers of the French Carmelites in Abbeville and in Cognac (where I prepared my talks). I must admit, however, that when I went into that office marked "Retreat Master" I didn't feel very sure of myself. (LL, 10)

At the end of that retreat, the superior of Our Lady's Missionaries offered L'Arche a nearby property. Steve and Ann Newroth returned to Canada from France to found the L'Arche Daybreak community in Richmond Hill, Ontario in 1969. Thus the second L'Arche community began as an interdenominational community of Anglicans, United Church members, and Roman Catholics. Over the next decades it would welcome Jewish and Muslim members as well.

Also, from that first retreat, "Faith and Sharing" in Canada and the United States was born, a movement to

organize retreats of the same kind. I would go to cities
where I had been invited and after the retreat a group was
appointed to prepare a similar retreat the following year.
It was often after such retreats that new L'Arche communities were born. ... As I reread our history, I realize how
important these retreats have been for me personally and
for L'Arche. (*LL*, 11)

In a way, Vanier's sense of the Christian church and other
faiths evolved alongside his growing appreciation of the di-
versity, specific gifts, and struggles of human beings. Like the
variety of people, so the variety of religious expression moved
Vanier and shaped his understanding of community and of God.

In 1969, Vanier traveled to India to explore the possibility
of beginning a L'Arche community there. The trip changed him,
opening him to a wider world, and to his own yearnings for
justice and peace in an even more intense way.

My trips to India that began in 1969 deeply marked my
life. I discovered a whole world of poverty that I had
never seen before in my life. At the time of the Civil War
in Bangladesh, I visited Calcutta and met Mother Teresa
and her sisters; hundreds of thousands of refugees were
flooding into India. ...

In India, I also discovered the vision and work of Mahatma Gandhi, especially his spirituality. In him I found a
prophet for our times, a man of God, a man of prayer, a
man deeply concerned about the life of the poor who saw
the "untouchables" as *harijans,* children of God. Gandhi
was concerned with peace and unity, a man ready to
risk his life in nonviolence, which for him was a spiritual reality rather than a political one. This man had a
whole vision of the land, of villages, life, and manual work
which was quite different from that of our modern society.
Gandhi marked my life deeply: he opened my mind and
enlarged my consciousness. (*ARK*, 55–56)

His excitement radiates off the pages of his letters. "I sense all that is happening within me. I feel impatient. How urgent it is for men of peace to rise up in our world," he writes.

The first L'Arche community in India opened in 1970. Vanier wrote of the community's fragility, with no prototype showing them how to build a community with handicapped people who were Hindu. "How should we eat, sing, and pray together?" he asks. The prayer room had a candle, incense, and "Gurunathan has put an image of his god in the prayer room (his brother said that they are all images of the same God)." They sang the Our Father and the prayer of L'Arche. "I love the way Guru kisses the earth in adoration," Vanier confides.

Mother Teresa of the Sisters of Charity encouraged and befriended Vanier. Her friendship and community model helped Vanier name the importance of the body in L'Arche as well: "She understood the mystery of the body, how touching and tending a broken person could lead to a real encounter."

In his retreats and public talks in North America and elsewhere, Vanier spoke of his experiences in India, seeing his own culture and assumptions with new critical distance. His travels also drew Vanier into a new kind of writing, with creative suggestions and occasional ironic questions. In a 1971 essay titled "I Wonder Why" Vanier comments:

> Do you think any social innovations are possible until we wage war against publicity — that form of publicity we see over television and in magazines — inciting to buy, using all forms of trickery (psychological and otherwise) and lies in order to incite people to buy. What would happen if instead of commercials we had "value-ads," inciting people to break down prejudices, to pardon faults, to seek universal brotherhood? (*IWW*, 18–19)

Faith and Light Begins

Vanier's experience brought him more and more in touch with the suffering and courage of the families of people with intellectual handicaps. In the late 1960s, a French woman named Marie-Hélène Matthieu and Vanier began planning a pilgrimage to Lourdes for people with handicaps, their parents, and friends. The impetus was the disturbing experience of a family with two boys with mental and physical disabilities. They were shunned by hotels in Lourdes, and the hotel that finally allowed them to stay required them to eat in their rooms to avoid disturbing other guests. Lourdes is, of course, a place of consolation, prayer, and healing for those in need: the family was deeply hurt by the rejection they experienced in such a holy place.

Matthieu and Vanier proposed an international pilgrimage to Lourdes for people with disabilities, their parents, and their friends. "In L'Arche we had discovered the importance of making pilgrimages together," Vanier explained. "The Jewish people, the Muslim people, the Hindu people as well as the Christian people, throughout the centuries have always had a deep sense of pilgrimage." Planning groups began in many countries.

Easter 1971 brought twelve thousand pilgrims from fifteen countries to Lourdes. Vanier describes it as "an important time of celebration and joy." The event was created not just to include the weakest and most vulnerable, but to make them the guests of honor, at the center of all the events. "For many parents it was a discovery that they were not alone, that their son or daughter was not a source of shame, and that they could celebrate together" (*LL*, 11).

The days of singing, praying, and building relationships concluded with a giant fiesta on the esplanade.

Planning and traveling had been done in local groups. Matthieu and Vanier suggested these groups stay in contact "and suddenly Faith and Light turned from a one-time pilgrimage into an international organization." Faith and Light and

L'Arche have close connections, part of a family. In 2008, there are fifteen hundred Faith and Light communities in eighty countries.

Expansion, Exhaustion, and New Choices

As interest in L'Arche and Faith and Light spread, Vanier traveled internationally to new communities, meetings, retreats, and formation events. His letters describe daily life, friends, and the cultural and political history and current events of India, Haiti, Brazil, Honduras, Guatemala, Ivory Coast, Poland, Italy, Australia, New Zealand, Northern Ireland and Ireland, Papua New Guinea, Lebanon, and Israel. He traveled at least once a year to Canada, speaking at universities, at retreats, and in prisons in both Canada and the United States.

A long trip in 1974 began in Haiti, then continued on to the United States, where Vanier met with people who were beginning L'Arche communities in Mobile, Alabama; Cleveland, Ohio; and Clinton, Iowa. Vanier visited communities in Erie, Pennsylvania, Vancouver, Victoria, Calgary, Edmonton, and Winnipeg, as well as meeting members of seven Eastern Canada communities, commenting, "I feel happy but a bit overwhelmed by all that is happening."

He led a conference with Wolf Wolfensberger, a professor from Syracuse whose articulation of "normalization," integrating people from institutional life back into society, was gaining international attention. Vanier was attentive to all the important movements of the times, and Wolfensberger became "a great friend of L'Arche."

On the same trip, after visiting three Canadian federal prisons, Vanier led a "Prison in Canada" weekend in Ottawa. The 170 participants included ex-prisoners, chaplains, prison visitors, rehabilitation officers, judges, lawyers, psychiatrists, prison directors, and administrators. Most interesting, participants were identified only by name, so in small group discussions no one knew the role or work of the others. The group met as human beings, and Vanier gave a talk on the pain, anguish, and fear prisoners can have, and how difficult it is for them to have a positive self-image. Vanier often tells audiences that if he had been born in other circumstances, he could have found himself in prison, full of the frustration and anger common to humans. In a letter to his communities at the end of his intense five-week trip, Vanier expressed shock that Canada could be open to the acceptance of people with handicaps, but in regression in regards to prisoners. "Prisons," he noted, "are not therapeutic."

By 1977, seventeen more L'Arche communities had begun in the United States and Canada, three in Belgium, five in France, two in the U.K., two in Scandinavia, and seven in Haiti, Honduras, Africa, and India.

A reader of Vanier's letters to L'Arche communities and friends through the 1970s cannot help but notice Vanier's growing exhaustion. The crowds in India became overwhelming rather than energizing. The suffering he sees weighs him down. It comes as no surprise when his letter dated April 18, 1976, begins, "Dear Friends, I am still in Cochin Hospital [France] with a bit of a fever."

In language often used by Vanier himself, times of "breakage," or "passages," are key points of integration and growth. His letters from the hospital were cheerful. After a few uncomfortable days, the staff promised to bring their tall patient "de Gaulle's bed." To Vanier's amused delight, it actually was an extra-long hospital bed, acquired when his parents' old friend, French president Charles de Gaulle, was a patient. Père Thomas's "quiet, prayerful presence" helped Vanier get through the long days. In his very constricted setting, he found kindness and community with his roommate, Saco, who shared any treats his friends brought him and gave Vanier massages when he was in pain. "Sometimes on sleepless nights," Vanier confides in an April 27 letter, "I think of men and women in their prison cells. I think of all the lonely people, and I realize how spoiled I am with so many who love me." He asks his community to remember in prayer the many lonely people hidden in prisons, hospitals, and solitary dwellings.

> My own experience of sickness strengthened this vision of the poor at the heart of L'Arche and as the heart of the church. On my return from India in 1976, I fell sick and had to be hospitalized. I had some intestinal infection, but above all, I was completely exhausted. Two months of impoverishment due to illness taught me a great deal. Jesus used this time to renew me spiritually. It was also an invitation for me to rest, and to pay more attention to my body and the pace of my life. (*FBC*, 58)

In all, Vanier spent two months in the hospital. During the three further months he spent recovering, Vanier made two retreats and discovered the charism of another Christian community, the Foyers de Charité in Montreal, and of Marthe Robin, who carried L'Arche in her heart and prayers.

In an interview later that year, Vanier spoke of the value of slowing down:

> Let us simply stop and start listening to our own hearts. There we will touch a lot of pain. We will possibly touch a lot of anger. We will possibly touch a lot of loneliness and anguish. Then we will hear something deeper. We will hear the voice of Jesus; we will hear the voice of God. We will discover that the heart of Christ, in some mysterious way, is hidden in my heart and there, we will hear, "I love you. You are precious to my eyes and I love you." (*ILWH*, 82)

He returned to his role as director of L'Arche in Trosly-Breuil, with an assistant director now carrying more responsibility. A letter written from Honduras shortly after Vanier resumed traveling suggests other ways in which Vanier was changed by his illness. He highlights in a new way the importance of spending spontaneous, unscheduled time with people. His own experience of being assisted in his weakness underlies a new sensitivity to the problematic aspects of L'Arche's distinction between the assisted and the assistants: "Everything I see here makes me really question our L'Arche communities and the double culture of the 'assistants' and the 'assisted' that can exist."

In March 1980, Vanier was again in Honduras when Archbishop Oscar Romero was murdered in nearby El Salvador. "The death of Archbishop Romero in San Salvador has shaken the country," he wrote to his community, "people are afraid." Vanier was in Choluteca to give a retreat that day and was asked to give the homily at the official Mass for Romero at the cathedral. Vanier spoke of Romero as "a man of peace who identified himself with the poor and who preached non-violence and reconciliation." Even when both the extreme right and the extreme left hated him, Romero was, like Jesus, not afraid to speak the truth. "It was a grace for me to speak of Romero," Vanier told his community.

In the autumn of 1980, Vanier stepped down from his role as community director and moved to live for a "sabbatical year" in La Forestière, a L'Arche home in Trosly for ten men and women with profound physical disabilities. The time of living with people who needed constant attention was one of peace and tenderness, a time of physical companionship and simplicity that nourished Vanier's soul. It was also one of the hardest years of his life. He grew to love his friends at La Forestière and they pushed him to grow. Vanier vividly described an important aspect of his experience:

> In 1980, when I left the role of community leader in Trosly, I lived a year at La Forestière.... The pitch of Lucien's scream was piercing and seemed to penetrate the very core of my being, awakening my own inner anguish. ... It was as if a part of my being that I had learned to control was exploding. It was not only Lucien's anguish that was difficult for me to accept but the revelation of what was inside my own heart — my capacity to hurt others. I

who had been called to share my life with the weak, had a
power of hatred for a weak person! (*BTS*, 61–63)

Vanier's time in the hospital and living in La Forestière
opened for him a more personal articulation of how L'Arche
is "founded on the body." He became more able to speak of
his own suffering, and the importance of each person recognizing their own "hidden places of pain.... Little by little we can
become a friend of our weakness."

Vanier tries to unpack the dynamic by which people can
choose to be open to transformation:

> Their cry for love flows also from their deep loneliness and
> their lack of self-esteem. They have called me to listen and
> to respond to their cry with competence, to welcome their
> vulnerability with tenderness, and then to be in commu-
> nion with them. As we respond to this fundamental cry
> for friendship, they begin to transform and to heal us. We
> can either hide our vulnerability behind a strong, protec-
> tive ego, or else we can discover that our vulnerability is a
> source of communion and unity.... In this way they have
> awoken in me what is deepest and most precious: a desire
> to give life to others and to receive life from them through
> a communion of hearts. (Unpublished talk)

Vanier has always treated the deepest secret of each human
heart with reverence and respect. The spiritual life is, Vanier
insisted, enormously important for people living in community.

> We all have to find our own rhythm of prayer.... In our
> deepest selves, below the levels of action and understand-
> ing, there is a vulnerable heart, a child who loves but is
> afraid to love. Silent prayer nourishes this deep place. It is
> the most important nourishment of all for people who live
> in community, because it is the most secret and personal.
> (*CG*, 190–91)

Throughout the next two decades, Vanier continued to re-
fine his understanding, from the silence of our hearts to specific

and historical political and social contexts. He worked with the international council of L'Arche, continuing to travel and give retreats.

His letters reveal how often Vanier happened to be in specific places during significant moments in their history. Vanier, the son of skilled diplomats, was attentive to the political and cultural context, the large historical significance, and the reality for people of all economic classes and abilities. In May of 1968, L'Arche members felt both concern and hope as more than ten million people went on strike across France. Vanier was in India in 1971 immediately after the tidal wave that killed twenty-five thousand people. With Mother Teresa, he visited refugee camps for the millions left homeless and was a close observer the next month as war broke out between India and Pakistan. Vanier was in Quebec during the Quiet Revolution. He visited Latin America at the height of the repression of the church, South Africa during apartheid, Lebanon during its civil war, the USSR in 1989 as it entered transition, the West Bank during the first Intifada, and the Philippines at the birth of democracy there. Talks in Pakistan were canceled during the 1991 Gulf War, and the L'Arche community in Bethany had to close. A 2008 letter is written from Kenya in the aftermath of their turbulent elections and unrest. And that is only a partial list!

In each of these unique circumstances and dramatic historical contexts, Vanier searched for a common understanding of what it is to be part of a global community. In a 1996 essay about his old friend Dan Berrigan, Vanier offered a description of a peacemaker engaged in the world:

> We need peacemakers like Daniel Berrigan everywhere, every day, in our families and in our cities and our churches, our places of work and our places of fun. We need peacemakers like Dan today in Bosnia and Rwanda, just as we needed Dan and others during the Vietnam war. We need people who love like Dan. To love is to reveal the hidden beauty in the hearts of all people, to trust them and to call

them forth to greater trust. To love is a way of looking, of touching, of listening to all: taking time with them, especially with those who are broken, depressed, and insecure, revealing to them their importance. As we take time with them and enter into communion with them, they in turn reveal to us our beauty. Communion is a to-and-fro of love; we give and receive mutually. We give our hearts bonded in gentle unity as words flow into silence and inner voice, as movement flows into quiet peace and inner rest. Life flows from one to another....

As we approach people in pain, they reveal to us our pain and brokenness. We are not an elite. We need help. We need the help of Jesus and of sisters and brothers in community; we need to talk to wise, listening, and compassionate hearts who can help us to assume all that is broken within us and to find wholeness. We become free when we accept ourselves as we are, cry out for help, and use wisely all that we are to build peace. (RFP, 134–35)

The 1990s ended with some significant personal changes for Vanier. In 1971, Pauline Vanier had moved to Trosly, where for the next twenty years she fed homesick Canadians tea and artichokes, befriended visitors such as Henri Nouwen, and grandmothered the entire community. She died in France in 1991, aged ninety-two, with her children around her. She was buried beside her husband in the Citadelle in Quebec. Georges and Pauline Vanier have been formally nominated for beatification in the Roman Catholic Church in recognition of their "love for humanity, deep spirituality, and propagation of Roman Catholic values."

Père Thomas "stayed at the heart of L'Arche for twenty-eight years," Vanier wrote after Père Thomas's death in 1993. He is buried near the chapel at La Ferme in Trosly-Breuil. "He was like a gentle and humble representative of God among us, full of compassion for all the members of the community, above all for those who were weakest and suffered most." Reflecting in 2007 on death, Vanier wrote, "In many ways his life epitomized that of L'Arche itself, and for some time after his death I couldn't speak of him without weeping because the union between us had been so deep. His death, however, was not an end: life and L'Arche continue to flow with all he has given and gives."

Well-known writer and priest Henri Nouwen lived in L'Arche for the last decade of his life before his sudden death in 1996. In a 1997 review of Nouwen's book *The Inner Voice of Love: A Journey through Anguish to Freedom,* Vanier explains why the famous professor and thinker found a genuine home in L'Arche:

> I had the privilege of knowing Henri Nouwen well. We met in 1981–82. We shared together, prayed together, and a deep friendship was born between us. In August 1985, he came to the community of Trosly-Breuil, France, for one year. After that time, he chose to go and live at Daybreak in Canada as the pastoral minister for the community.
>
> What struck me about Henri during those first years was, on the one hand, his deep human and spiritual insights, and on the other, the cry of his whole being for friendship; he seemed to live an intolerable loneliness. I soon began to realize that these two aspects were bonded together. His spiritual insights flowed from his own inner pain.
>
> Healing does not come from outside a person but from inside: medication is for the stimulation of the healing forces within the body. A healer is one who activates and calls forth these healing forces within a wounded person, through the transmission of love, of trust, and of hope. A healer acts not through imposition of law, but by attraction: the attraction to life and of life. To be healed one must want to live and to give life, not just to escape from suffering and to be comfortable.
>
> People with mental handicaps are beautiful, though also demanding and disturbing wounded healers. Is that not why Henri, himself a wounded healer, was attracted to them? Did he not see his own face and wounded

heart in their faces and wounded hearts? ("Listening to a 'Wounded Healer' in the Search for Life," *Catholic New Times*, February 23, 1997, p. 17)

In 1998, Jean Vanier broadcast across Canada his evolving thinking about what it means to be human as that year's Massey lecturer, commissioned by the Canadian Broadcasting Corporation and Massey College at the University of Toronto. The five popular talks framed Vanier's unique "anthropology" and became a best-selling book titled *Becoming Human*.

Beginning the Twenty-First Century

As the new century began, Vanier turned his attention to two main areas that had always been deeply part of L'Arche: youth and peacemaking. He traveled speaking specifically to youth, encouraging their idealism and intuition, urging them to understand suffering and happiness, sharing stories from his life, offering them the trust and confidence that his father offered him so long ago.

After September 11, 2001, Vanier wrote a short, heartfelt book titled *Finding Peace,* noting, "The events of September 11 called me to become personally committed to peacemaking, to continue to reflect on peace and on the sources of violence in our world, in me, and in each one of us." He was simultaneously moved and thoughtful about the way in which people gathered to express desire and fear:

> People from various cultures and religions, as well as people with no specific religious tradition came together after the attacks to pray and to affirm together their vision of mutual acceptance and their esteem and love for all human beings. And yet the evenings of prayer I participated in left me a bit uneasy. I felt as though people were not praying for a new just order between people and nations, but, motivated by fear, were praying to keep the

status quo — no change, no insecurity, nothing that would disturb their lives or views on the world. (*FP*, 4–6)

For decades, Vanier had been exploring how human beings open themselves to change. Is insecurity the necessary path to finding the happiness that people and communities deeply desire? Vanier continued to ask what a "new just order" would look like, between individuals and between nations, and to develop a nuanced and unromanticized vision of community life. L'Arche itself reflected that tension between the security of the status quo, and the inescapable reality of insecurity:

> Our communities are always fragile because communion is always fragile. People are free to come and go from L'Arche. Although we hope that assistants will discover L'Arche as a call, there's no *rational* reason often for an assistant to stay.... This is how we love with freedom, but it also creates insecurity for our communities, and humans prefer security. L'Arche is a place where one is constantly growing — a journey together....
>
> And our communion is all we have: our security comes from communion, mutual trust, and God, not from our structures. We are free to say yes or no. Structures can evolve but only communion can deepen. (Unpublished talk)

As in 1964, L'Arche remains a sign of hope, and L'Arche also has matured as an organization, with a complex structure of responsibility and roles. Vanier insists that L'Arche is a journey, not an end in itself, and its life is always founded on freedom, not structures. Even when discussing the administration or future of L'Arche, Vanier circles back to universal questions of freedom, happiness, and what it is to be human.

His inspiration remains rooted in his relationships with people with intellectual disabilities, and his most profound insights into culture and humanness come through that perspective. Reflecting on the changes he has seen, Vanier observed five different attitudes in broader Western societies toward people with intellectual disabilities. He explains the first attitude as seeing disability as a sign of disorder, so that it has to be suppressed.

> Aristotle felt this. This attitude persists today as we see in the high rates of selective abortion of unborn babies who are diagnosed with a disability. For instance, now in France it is very difficult for women to choose to stay pregnant with a baby with Downs Syndrome due to the pressure on them from doctors to have an abortion. (Unpublished talk)

The second is frequently seen: this "so-called charitable attitude is marked by pity, and those who look after the poor are considered saints by the general public." The third attitude is when the public and professionals recognize with respect and compassion that people with disabilities are "really human beings who can grow and progress." This leads to competent and attentive care, integrated schools, work opportunities, and independent living. A fourth, though less common attitude Vanier suggests "has emerged from the third": the realization that "when you are in relationship with people with disabilities, something good can happen." Communion can begin and a genuine and even transformative friendship can be mutually enjoyed. Vanier chooses his words with care to describe the fifth attitude. "For some, there is a discovery that people with disabilities can lead them to God. They are a path to an experience of God. People with disabilities are necessary for the wholeness of the body, of humanity." This process, Vanier is quick to clarify, "is about humanizing disability, not spiritualizing it." He characterizes this kind of exploration as part of his anthropology, springing from his experience of human beings and the humanness of spirituality.

In 2007, Vanier reflected on how the public letters he wrote to his friends and communities had changed. As L'Arche grew, he had become conscious of writing to a wider audience and being given a wider perspective to share. He suggests this is true of "any real movement with real significance": it has to have a universal meaning, the sharing of a world vision to address our common humanity. "We weren't just sharing life with Christians, we were sharing life with people who were suffering; and if you're talking generally about people who are suffering, then you're talking about people everywhere," he explained.

The universality of Vanier's insights and the significance of L'Arche and Faith and Light have been recognized worldwide. His awards include Companion of the Order of Canada, the Legion of Honour (France), the Pope Paul VI International Prize, the International Peace Award (Community of Christ), the Rabbi Gunther Plaut Humanitarian Award, the Beacon Fellowship Prize, and the Gaudium et Spes Award. In presenting the International Paul VI Award in 1997, Pope John Paul II identified Vanier as "a great spokesman for the culture of solidarity and 'the civilization of love,' in the fields of both thought and action." He then recognized members of L'Arche, saying, "The distinction conferred today...particularly honours individuals with handicaps, from the first two whom Mr. Jean Vanier took into his home, to the great number of those who currently belong to L'Arche. Indeed they are the principal figures of L'Arche, who with faith, patience, and a fraternal spirit make it a sign of hope and a joyful witness."

Looking Ahead

Life is about growth, Vanier likes to say. Chronology cannot grasp the breadth of growth, because growth is difficult to value or pin down in a world of "when did this happen?"

> If I were to write an autobiography — to move through my life chronologically describing the things that have happened to me and the people I have met — it would not

be possible to explain the purpose and meaning of my life.
(*OJH*, xvi)

As he ages, Vanier says that, rather than "growing up," he
is now "growing downward." This includes "living with anguish without running away from it," and "acknowledging that
today I am weak and tired and I can't solve the problems of
others." He reflects: "I sense more and more the mystery of the
vulnerable God; the all-powerful one becomes the vulnerable
one." He is intentionally articulate about his own process of
growing older.

> I don't know how I will fare when I can't "do" anything
> for people anymore. Giving retreats, meeting with people
> in our communities and others in challenging situations
> all give me life. None of us knows that final passage of
> weakness and how we are going to live it.

> On the whole I can live quite peacefully today even though
> I know there is always anguish inside somewhere to be
> worked at. I am not good at dropping my barriers, but
> I do the best I can. Our humanity is so beautiful, but it
> needs to be transformed. We are called to live everyday life
> but also to be open to the events — the encounter or meet-
> ing that can be transformative and that gives me a sense of
> the resurrection that is possible for us. (Unpublished talk)

"People with disabilities have called forth the child in me,"
Vanier reveals. "They have taught us all in L'Arche how to rest
in love and mutual caring, how to celebrate life and also celebrate death, to speak about death, to accompany people who
are dying. Death is a part of life; it is not something to be
terrified about. It is the final passage into a new life."
His community looks after him and encourages him to rest,
in between his many continued travels around the world. Vanier
makes clear that he is sustained and inspired both by his life in
community, and by his prayer:

Maybe the secret of my life is the living day by day with people with intellectual disabilities. They are my strength, my source. This life together is a source of my word (retreats, conferences, etc.). But there is also the silence of being in communion with Jesus. (Personal letter)

In a book about the Gospel of John, published in 2004, Vanier explains his experience of prayerful silence, writing, "I have come to see that to pray is above all to dwell in Jesus and to let Jesus dwell in me." He continues:

Prayer is a place of rest and quiet.
When we love someone,
don't we love just to be with each other,
to be present one to another?
Now and again we may say a word of affection,
we will be attentive to each other and listen to each other,
but it is essentially a place of silence. (*DMJ*, 358)

Out of that silent communion with Jesus has come the extraordinary clarity of Vanier's universal and inclusive vision.

The future of the world is in the hands of each of us, and it depends on our commitment together with others for peace, each according to our own gifts and responsibilities. Peace is not a question of stopping this or that catastrophe, but of rediscovering a vision, a path of hope for all of humanity. (*FP*, 4–6)

Writings

Jean Vanier writes simply, in a pastoral and brotherly way, but with the horizons of someone who has traveled extensively and who probes with the precision of his training as a philosopher. For example, he does not just exhort his readers to forgive. He offers three principles and five steps toward forgiveness and distinguishes between forgiveness and reconciliation.

Vanier always probes deeper, under the surface experience to the dynamics beneath.

Vanier analyzes different levels of his themes. He sets out the literal level, describing, for example, the fear that blocks our ability to love or choose peace. The social level recognizes fear as a social and inculturated response to possible commitments and unknown implications. A psychological level notices how fears emerge from past wounds. An emotional level shows fear as a response to what another's anguish awakens in our own hearts. Every experience invites a spiritual level, as an invitation to relationship with God, held in the large picture of God's desire for the world.

Vanier's published work covers a remarkable variety of topics. He is known as a spiritual writer, but describes some of his work more as "an anthropology," exploring human society and choices. Rather like a singer with a five-octave range, Vanier addresses directly topics at which many spiritual writers would flinch. In a tone that is serious yet full of delight, he ponders washing dishes, leisure activities, and the complexity of human sexuality. He analyzes our society's approach to inclusion and exclusion, world peace and spiritual practices. His delight and respect for the complex, often messy, reality of human life shine through his writings on love of enemies, living in reality, the secret mystery of each human heart. From Gospel stories and prayer to activism to the roots of depression to rituals around death, few nonfiction writers can discuss comfortably such a concrete spectrum of human experience.

In all his writings, Vanier offers stories to grab a reader's imagination: Jewish and Palestinian young men walking together loved by their Jerusalem neighborhood; the woman in Rwanda who could not forgive but could choose not to wish violence upon the people who murdered her family; Claudia's long and complex journey to freedom; Vanier's own growth.

Vanier's sense of humor shines through, especially in books based on talks. He delightedly described to a Harvard audience the dangers of mutual flattery:

We are all so much in need of affection that when somebody gives it to us we want to hold on to it. Then we say to the other person, "You're wonderful! Keep at it! Keep flattering me! You know, it's nice." We're like little cats who need to be caressed. We then begin to purr. (*FBC*, 37)

To a large conference in Northern Ireland called "Encountering the Other," Vanier noted:

At the heart of the message of Jesus is "love your enemies, do good to those who hate you, speak well of those who speak evilly of you, pray for those who crush you and persecute you." It sounds beautiful. Have you ever tried to say something nice about somebody you know is criticizing you behind your back? Try to say something nice about that person. You'll find your glands will swell up.

(*EO*, 54)

With his eyes dancing, Vanier likes to tell the story of a visitor:

A man came to see me when I was director of the L'Arche community. He was a man with many problems: family problems, work problems, and philosophical problems. He was a very sad person. I suppose he was somebody very normal. I don't like the word "normal" but if anyone was normal, it was this man. While he was sharing his sadness with me there was a knock on the door, and before I could answer it, Jean Claude was in my office and laughing. Some people call Jean Claude mongoloid or Down's syndrome but we just call him Jean Claude. Jean Claude is a happy man. He likes to come by my office and shake my hand. And that is what he did. He shook my hand and laughed. Then he shook the hand of Mr. Normal and laughed and he walked out laughing. Mr. Normal looked at me and said, "Isn't it sad that there are children like that."

The great pain in all of this was that this man was totally blind. He had barriers inside of him and was unable to see that Jean Claude was happy. You couldn't find anyone more relaxed and happy than Jean Claude. Fundamentally, when people start lamenting because there are people with handicaps in our world, the question is whether it is more sad that there are people with handicaps or that there are people who reject them. Which is the greater handicap? Is it that there are men like Jean Claude or is it that Mr. Normal has this barrier which renders him totally blind to the beauty of people? (*ILWH*, 94–95)

His letters also radiate amusement, from floods to flat tires to rats eating sandals in India. In the hospital for two months with a mysterious tropical illness, Vanier writes to his community, "Alleluia! Since my last letter many beautiful things have happened. My temperature shot up, nearly breaking the thermometer, then a few days later shot down.... Of course, this worried the doctors and made them suspect that there must be a cause to all this" (*OLT*, 199).

Vanier's books have diverse origins, including talks given at retreats, lectures, public letters written to communities and friends, and extended meditations on specific themes. In some of his books, the text is broken into phrases and spaced so that it looks like poetry. He calls this distinctive style "meditative prose."

A Note about the Structure of This Book

This book is about transformation. Perhaps counterintuitively, it moves from the large vision for the world, to community life, to the heart of each individual. That has been the movement of Vanier's own life.

Vanier's transformation was not from psychological or spiritual maturity to community responsibility to global awareness and commitment. Rather, for Vanier, the movement was reversed. Born into a Canadian diplomatic family with a strong global sense of public service, coming of age in Europe during World War II, Vanier was intensely aware of political and global realities. Leaving his military career in his twenties, he lived in a community of theological students from around the world. In his thirties, he was moved by the Gospels and his spiritual mentor to begin an unusual community, inviting two men with intellectual disabilities to live with him permanently. Through their friendship, Vanier's own heart was transformed and his understanding of himself deepened and became more honest.

Thus, for Vanier, the movement was from global consciousness to community life to personal change. Many current spiritual and self-help books assume that we must do deep inward work first to change ourselves and reach a certain level of self-awareness, and then move outward into engagement in wider society. The problem is that many people do not move beyond their inner-work stage, being both self-absorbed and self-aware enough to know they have a long way to go still. Their moment of leadership and responsibility is endlessly delayed. Vanier's experience tells readers that to take responsibility and do our best in community will change our hearts and our world.

Jean Vanier famously says, "Change the world, with love, one heart at a time." This book is shaped around these three movements of transformation:

1. Change the world: transformation of society, of our global community

2. With love: transformation through relationships, through community

3. One heart at a time: transformation of the human person, of our hearts.

Chapter 4 delves more deeply into the human heart through Vanier's writings about prayer, retreat, and his spiritual life as a Christian. A final short epilogue offers a summary of Vanier's vision, because always the transformation of the heart will bring us back into a passionate engagement with our world today.

Our human work is not simply internal growth or accepting our humanness. We each have something to offer. Vanier returns to his foundational reading of philosophy, noting, "The vision of the ancients was to have a mission for eternity. Everything dies but all have the mission to transmit life. This is the meaning of life."

Several years after my family and I left L'Arche, I was talking with Vanier about my own mission and my continued uncertainty. "I wonder if we left too soon," I confided. "I've done interesting work since we moved, but I miss our L'Arche family." To my surprise, Jean Vanier laughed out loud and took my face in his big hands. His merry eyes met mine, and he called me by my family nickname with respect and tenderness, "Ah, Carrie, *beware nostalgia*."

What an unexpected response. It was one of those prophetic moments that you wake up for. There is something in that moment that sums up Vanier for me — the direct engagement, the cheerful confidence in each person's freedom and ability to create something beautiful, the practical insistence on living in reality. In reading these selections from Vanier's writings, I hope you will catch something of that spirit. Perhaps you will find a desire to grow, to explore new ways to engage and transmit life. But if you find yourself imagining that you must follow a path scripted elsewhere, then...beware nostalgia!

Acknowledgments

My heartfelt thanks to Jean Vanier, who was pleased with this project from the beginning and offered me his confidence generously. I am grateful for his friendship over many years. Robert Ellsberg of Orbis Books initiated this edition of Orbis's Modern Spiritual Masters series: through the process, we have become friends. Kevin Burns of Novalis Press answered my many questions with unfailing good humor. Julia Wolf read through piles of possible material and recommended themes and structure. Flavia Silano provided valuable editorial insights for the Introduction. Anne Osler sent me several books that were difficult to access. John Dear sustained me with cheerful and frequent encouragement. Jeff Moore kindly spent a day housebound by a snowstorm digging out his excellent photos of Vanier and more time getting the beautiful cover photo scanned. My thanks to Gabrielle Earnshaw and Anna St. Onge at the Henri Nouwen Archives at the University of St. Michael's College, University of Toronto. The heart illustration used throughout the book was inspired by the dynamic hearts that Francis Maurice of L'Arche Daybreak designed and by a sketch of concentric hearts that Greg Lannan of L'Arche Toronto once drew for me. Barbara Swanekamp was responsive and helpful in early stages: we are all sorry she died before seeing the final book. Christine McGrievy's suggestions and insights improved the Introduction. My beloved Geoff Whitney-Brown contributed hours of his time to type in text, at least twice as much as was finally included. Janet, Monica, and David Whitney-Brown understand community and forgiveness even better after sharing their home and mother with this project: their support has been tremendous. I am deeply grateful to all of you.

1

"Change the World..."
Transformation of Society

This first chapter, "Change the world..." begins with Vanier's reflections on the urgent task of peacemaking from his own history and experience. Excerpts of talks Vanier has addressed to specific audiences follow: these give a sense of Vanier's ability to be direct, simultaneously challenging and in solidarity as a fellow-seeker. Important to our global community are faith issues: Vanier discusses personal experiences and his hopes for greater ecumenism and interfaith friendship. The chapter concludes with Vanier's reflections on the teaching of Jesus that "if it had been followed, would have changed the history of the world: Love your enemies."

PEACEMAKING

I joined the royal navy in 1942, when I was thirteen. I crossed the Atlantic at a time when one ship in five was being sunk. Before going I went to my father, and I asked him if I could join the navy. He asked "Why?" I don't remember my answer; what I remember is that he said, "I trust you. If that is what you want, you must do it. I trust you: So for me the whole question of peacemaking is centered on trust. Trust that you are important, that you are precious, that you have something important to give to the world, to give to me. If we don't believe we are precious, what happens? We have anguish."

For me, the message of the Gospel is that each one of us has a gift to give; each one is precious; each one needs to be loved and to belong.

The fundamental principle of peace is a belief that each person is important. Even if you cannot speak, even if you cannot walk, even if you've been abandoned, you have a gift to give to the other. Do you believe you are important? Do you believe — do we all believe — that we can do something to make this world a better place? Why is the gap between the rich and the poor, the powerful and the powerless growing? There can be no peace unless we can become aware of where this growing gap comes from.   —*EO,* 11–13

I recall the 6th of August 1945. I was in the navy then, and I still remember those pictures of the incredible mushroom that came up over Hiroshima and then three days later Nagasaki. We became very conscious of the capacity of humanity to destroy itself. Not long ago I was in Japan, and I took the opportunity to go to Hiroshima to the Memorial of Peace, which in reality is a memorial of war. I saw the pictures of the devastation of just one bomb where more than one hundred thousand people were killed. I think that today humanity is conscious that with thirty thousand nuclear missiles and warheads we are able to destroy all of life.

That is why I feel that the fundamental lesson that human beings should be given is how to become men and women of peace so they can become men and women of hope. Today conflict is very dangerous to our spirit. When I use the word "conflict," I am not only talking about war or armaments. I am referring to more subtle forms of conflict, such as when a person with a handicap is not listened to or when he or she is put into an institution and there not helped to develop. That too, is conflict; that is crushing people. People everywhere are being oppressed.

We see this in the West Bank, in South Africa, in North America, in South America and China, and in individual people who have been rejected. They are being held down and their life is not being allowed to evolve. — *ILWH,* 20

I came to the little village of Trosly-Breuil in France in 1964. There I met men who had been wounded in their minds and in their psyches when they were young. It was there that I felt called to open up a small home for other men like them...and so it was that the adventure of L'Arche began.

Living with Raphaël and Philippe and many others who have become my brothers and sisters, I began to understand a little better the message of Jesus and his particular love for the poor in spirit and for the impoverished and weak ones of our society. I have learned much from them and feel deeply indebted to them. They have shown me what it is to live simply, to love tenderly, to speak in truth, to pardon, to receive openly, to be humble in weakness, to be confident in difficulties, and to accept handicaps and hardships with love. And, in a mysterious way, in their love they have revealed Jesus to me.

I had met Jesus before. He had called me from a career in the navy to a life of prayer and metaphysics, a life also where I loved living simply and poorly, available to the Spirit. But it was only when I came to L'Arche that I really met and lived with men who were despised and rejected. It is there that I discovered also in a new way all those barriers in myself which cause me to despise and to reject others who are of different ways and opinions.

It was there that I discovered the two worlds that exist side by side: the world of the "normal" people, who seek social status and are motivated by ambitions of efficiency and riches, and the "abnormal" world of the despised, the handicapped, the "not-adapted-ones," be they prisoners, prostitutes, or mentally sick.

I began to see the deep wounds caused by the lack of compassion of the "normal" and "good" people; I began to sense the fear that seemed to motivate them.

And then I went to India where with some friends we were able to start up a small home for handicapped people. There I discovered the beauty, the grandeur, the nobility and the simplicity of the Indian culture. Of course, I also saw much poverty. But maybe I was more struck by the interior poverty in the West. When I returned to Europe I felt deeply the squandering of riches, the hardness of hearts, and the egotistical materialism of so many of the "developed" countries.

While in India, I learned to love Gandhiji, feeling that he is one of the great prophets of our times. His deep love for the underprivileged, especially the untouchables; his desire to identify himself with them; his openness to the spirit of God in order to become an instrument of his peace; his desire to unite men, particularly those of opposed religions; his universal heart; his deep desire to bring peace into the world; his vision of poverty and riches; his own poverty; all these attracted me deeply. Gandhiji seemed to follow so authentically the Sermon on the Mount and the Beatitudes, those Beatitudes which seem to have been for him in many ways a guiding light. Far from separating me from Jesus, Gandhiji seemed to bring me closer to him, teaching me much about his gentleness and his tenderness. The Beatitudes of the meek seems to be none other than the deep strength, the peace, the patience and unceasing goodness and love of nonviolence, *ahimsa,* about which Gandhiji spoke so often. Gandhiji taught me to love Jesus more and gave me a desire to make my life more like his, especially in this domain of a struggle for peace and universal brotherhood. And this struggle can be won only by using the means of the Spirit: those of love, of gift of self, of gentleness, with no aggression or violence.

—*EH,* "Preface"

I am becoming more and more aware of the vast divisions in our world and of the prejudices and hatred which cultivate them. Groups tend to look down upon one another, feeling that they are the best, the wisest, and the strongest. In every continent and country there are oppressed and minority groups: the

Aborigines in Australia, the tinkers in Ireland, the untouchables in India, immigrants in England, Puerto Ricans in the States, and so on. It seems that every group, in order to feel it exists, must relate to another group that it considers inferior.

The same is true of each person. Very quickly each one wants to prove that he or she is right and the other wrong. A whole system of competition and success, so deeply ingrained in Western civilization, is based on the need to prove that "I am better than you."

But alas, if one person or group has the elation of victory, the other has the depression of defeat. For everyone that wins a prize there are many losers. And this brings much depression, for the losers are left with the feeling of inferiority. So it is that our world becomes quickly divided into those who have power and success and those who feel broken. Some have too much, others very little. Those who have quickly condemn those who have little; these in turn are left with a broken self-image; they tend to condemn themselves.

One of the serious needs in our world today is to learn to walk with our aggression. So often instead of dealing with our negative feelings directly we direct them toward others who are innocent....

Our modern world has fantastic power and knowledge. Man has conquered the moon, delved into the secret of matter, and discovered immense energies. Yes, we have amazing knowledge. But the only real knowledge necessary for the survival of the human race is lacking: the knowledge of how to transform violence and hatred into tenderness and forgiveness; how to stop the chain of aggression against the weak; how to see differences as a value rather than as a threat; how to stop people from envying those who have more and incite them to share with those who have less. The real question of today is disarmament, not only on the international scale but in terms of our own personal aggression. Is it possible for men and women to break down the barriers of prejudice and fear that separates groups and races and to create one people? Are we condemned to war, or is peace possible?   — *CLA*, 256–57

Peace brings into one body the rich and the poor, the inwardly broken and the outwardly broken. Jesus has a vision for our world: to bring to birth societies and communities that are not first of all a pyramid of power — with the rich, the privileged, and the powerful on the top, and the poor, the useless, and the powerless on the bottom — but a body, where the weak and the strong support each other, are there for each other, and give life to one another.

It is not easy, however, for the poor to rise up from the ruins of their existence to claim life and responsibility for themselves, to find hope and new laughter. It is not easy for the rich to allow themselves to be touched by the poor, to enter into communion with them, to let themselves be stripped of luxury and comfort. No, it is not easy for the rich and for the poor to sit down together at the same table.

And yet Jesus says to us:

When you give a lunch or dinner, do not invite your friends or your relations or rich neighbors, in case they invite you back and repay you. No, when you have a party, invite the poor, the crippled, the lame, the blind; then you will be blessed. (Luke 14:12–15)

To eat at the same table is to become friends. The vision of Jesus is to break down the dividing walls of hostility and prejudice that separate people and to bring them together in love. But the poor are wounded and angry, fearful and depressed. They disturb. Their anger disturbs. The rich too are wounded and fearful, hiding behind barriers of self-satisfaction and power. Communities of faith, of God's reign, bring together into oneness those who by culture and by education are far apart. This is the body of Christ. This is the church. The poor are evangelized. They discover they are loved. But even more, the poor evangelize. They possess a healing power that awakens and transforms the hearts of the rich.   — *RFP,* 133

If we enter into personal relationships
with those who are weak and lonely
— not just to do good to them but to be with them —
then we enter into a personal relationship with God.
And as we begin to celebrate life together
so we discover the heart of God.

Many of us were taught
"an eye for an eye, a tooth for a tooth."
This is the general rule in many of our societies.
It is normal to want to protect oneself
and to respond to aggression with aggression or repression.
Yet Jesus tells us
   "Love your enemies
   Do good to those who hate you (Matt 5:44).
   Let go of your defense mechanisms.
   You do not need to protect yourselves
   for I am your protection."

Hope for our world lies not
in the manufacture of greater weapons
or the implementation of more repressive laws;
hope lies in our capacity to love and to forgive
and in our desire to live reconciliation
and to grow in love for our enemies.   — *BTS*, 86

TALKS TO SPECIFIC AUDIENCES

In these five speeches spanning twenty years, Vanier addresses specific audiences with sympathetic frankness. He calls on elected political representatives to avoid building themselves up by humiliating their opponents. He urges religious superiors to address the wealth of their congregations. To the elite Empire Club, he names the dangers of comfort, power, and security. The Vanier Institute of the Family is urged to think beyond traditional definitions of "family." He announces to a Harvard audience that

healing is found at the bottom of the ladder. In each situation,
Vanier speaks as a brother, as a fellow-pilgrim who understands
and is also wrestling with the dilemmas and contradictions unique
to each audience.

Speech delivered at National Prayer Breakfast for members of the Canadian Parliament and others, June 7, 1967, during the days of the Israeli-Arab Six-Day War

The world is going through one of the deepest and gravest crises of its history. This present crisis is one of transition. We are leaving an era of smug complacency for one of rapid change and technological innovations.

This crisis is affecting all our lives, affecting our society and our families, and it is coupled with deep distress and anxiety. Many, at the sight of so much evil, strife and war, are wondering if man is not only thoroughly stupid but also fundamentally evil. We talk about peace and unity, but how many men today throughout our world are, on the contrary, either at war or actually preparing for war? We know full well the possibilities of destruction that are in our hands....

I beg that each one of us today may take stock of the seriousness of the situation and the gravity of our own responsibilities. Will it not be in prayer that we can find the vision necessary to disentangle ourselves from the immediate and to look forward to the future; to have the vision and the insight necessary to see how we can orient humanity to real goals of justice, friendship and fraternity? Will it not be in prayer that we will find the strength necessary to remain faithful to our convictions? ... And so, my friends, may we take stock at this Prayer Breakfast. In a few moments, we will return to our occupations, perhaps uttering hard, humiliating words, frequently trying to break others in order to gain power. Let us take stock of our presence here. The grandeur of the occasion, the sublimity of the prayers, do they not oblige us to reflect upon what all this means and implies? May I suggest that there may be a danger that in a few minutes we will be back on the floor of the House with slaughtering words, back in industry or in our professions with quick and sometimes cruel reactions. Of course, competition, hard discussion, are vital necessities to free government and private enterprise. The party system is an excellent source of valid and thoughtful action, but how often do we speak only to wound the opponent, to slay him, defame him, make him a laughing stock. How eager we are to profit from every opportunity to humiliate. Power attained through humiliating others, and not through the radiation of one's own personal goodness and wisdom and foresight carries the seeds of its own destruction.

— *EH*, 66–68

Talk given to major superiors of religious orders, Toronto, February 1969

This question of poverty is not easy, especially in regards to riches that belong to communities, collective riches. Nobody seems to answer for them. They belong to the group, and we know that after we leave there will be another group that will be responsible. When one person accepts all the responsibility then he can be pinned down. You can say to him, "Why do you do this? Is this according to the Gospel of Jesus? Answer me!" But with a group we cannot pin anybody down.

> Therefore I tell you, do not be anxious about your life, what you shall eat or what you shall drink, nor about your body, what you shall put on. Is not life more than food, and the body more than clothing? Look at the birds of the air: they neither sow nor reap nor gather into barns, and yet your heavenly Father feeds them. Are you not of more value than they? And which of you by being anxious can add one cubit to his span of life? And why are you anxious about clothing? Consider the lilies of the field, how they grow; they neither toil nor spin; yet I tell you, even Solomon in all his glory was not arrayed like one of these. But

if God so clothes the grass of the field, which today is alive and tomorrow is thrown into the oven, will he not much more clothe you, O men of little faith? Therefore do not be anxious, saying, "What shall we eat?" or "What shall we drink?" or "What shall we wear?" For the Gentiles seek all these things; and your heavenly Father knows that you need them all. (Matt. 6:25–32)

Nevertheless, with our heritage and with our personal and collective egotisms we do find ourselves in difficult situations. I felt it strongly when I was in Bombay recently. There are the most terrible slums there. People in the north of India from rural areas where there has been drought flock into the city in the hope of finding work. They lie on the pavements and then from the pavements they go into the slum areas where there is disease, malnutrition, serious poverty. Large families live in sheds — call them what you will — pieces of bamboo with banana leaves around them. When the rain comes, it pours in, sometimes destroying the shed.

Just across the street from one of these slum areas there is a large religious house where I had been invited to speak to the novices. We drove through beautiful gardens with large trees and lovely flowers. When I came up in front of the novitiate I was greeted by the priest superior, a really wonderful person. I was taken into the house and shown the spacious rooms of the novices. I had dinner with them. During the talk I asked them if they were not embarrassed by the slums in front of their house. I had never seen a situation like this. On the other side of the street, the dirt, the hovels, the misery, and on this side, a large property, spacious rooms, comfort, and food. What could be the spiritual formation of these men! Obviously each novice would have to build a barrier around his heart and his mind. How could he read the Gospels and stay on this side of the street?

The superior of the house was wondering how he could transform this novitiate into something which would have meaning in the Christian sense, so that the novices could enter into the world of the Beatitudes. He was wondering whether to bring in the dying and the sick. What should he do? But it was his hope, his anguish, and his confidence in the Spirit that really enthralled me. Not acting quickly out of impulse, but seeing the problem, anguishing about the problem, yet confident that the Spirit would show the solution if he continued to pray and to act and to talk with the novices. As one walks down the road and looks to the left and then to the right, one would wonder on which side of the road Jesus lives....

When you are rich, when you have a name, when you have friends, or when you are a member of a respected group, you are never really oppressed. When in difficulty, simply make a telephone call and everything is fixed. I know this myself. I've never been really poor because I have enough friends and contacts. When you have no friends, when you are an immigrant and you speak the language badly, you are quickly oppressed, for you cannot defend yourself.... You can be sure that the first question that is always brought up in any situation when one is talking with people who are worried about faith in Jesus is the question of finance. Who has the money? What image am I giving of Jesus and of his mystical body? Isn't it a terrible thing that the Poor One, the Crucified One, is thought to be with those who have surrounded themselves with comfort?

Our congregations have their own heritage and their traditions, and they are not easy to change. There are no easy formulas. But if we want to be meaningful to the world of today as witnesses of Jesus, sharing and continuing his life, we must ask ourselves if we are willing to be poor in order to be filled by the riches of his love.

> And a scribe came up and said to him, "Teacher, I will follow you wherever you go." And Jesus said to him, "Foxes have holes, and birds of the air have nests; but the Son of man has nowhere to lay his head." (Matt. 8:19–20)

> He who finds his life will lose it, and he who loses his life
> for my sake will find it. (Matt. 10:39)

> By this we may be sure that we are in him: he who says he
> abides, in him ought to walk in the same way in which he
> walked. (1 John 2:5–6)

The first and fundamental attitude is to remember that Jesus
loves us. He knows our faults and our weaknesses. He knows
the difficulties springing from ages past, and that we have in-
herited a whole way of life. Jesus is not brutal; he is loving.
But he is demanding, because he knows that the future of his
church, his spouse and his mystical body, depends on our openness and our freedom in the Holy Spirit. The Holy Spirit must
come into the details of our lives, and we must look to these details so that we can begin to change. It might be by giving away
those superfluous riches — because in all of our homes there are
superfluous riches, be they paintings or old pieces of furniture.
Money could go to the needy missions, to lands where people
are dying of hunger. If only each of our houses and congregations could begin by giving those things where there is no big
decision to be made! If only we realized, first of all, the suffering of the world; and the witnesses. If only we could allow him
to gradually deepen us and help us understand the problems
caused by large investments.   — FJ, 54–58

Talk given to the Empire Club of Canada, February 11, 1971

While we eat today...I think of the wounded and the despised
the world over, and of the children of India. Because of them, I
am beginning to sense the vast division of our world.

On one side, men hiding themselves in comfort and in security, the securities of wealth, of possessions, of clubs, and of
drink. Here we have in many ways the makers of this world:
those who have made good and are sitting on the crest of success. Their eyes are glued to wealth and domination and social

esteem. They may be men of morality or immorality; they may have had their way blessed, journeying more or less in harmony with religious groups. Their conscience may be clear because they have put a few bills in the beggar's hat that is offered to them from the poor quarters of their own city, or even from far-off countries. They live in a world of luxury, of superfluous goods, of snobbishness, of expensive houses and motor cars, of well-fed children with beautiful well-brushed hair and well-cleaned finger nails, who are going to good schools and are heading, maybe, toward the same crest of success where they, too, will be able to open bank accounts.

On the other side, another world, a world of the handicapped and of the broken, those who are on welfare, who slug down the streets or are shut up in prisons or psychiatric hospitals, who may have taken to drugs and drink and prostitution. Go to the big homes for the mentally and physically handicapped, the psychiatric hospitals and the prisons, and find out where you might be if you had had that sickness or virus at the age of four, if you had been hit by a cyclist when very young, or if you had been born in a world of squalor and violence. You will see then what I mean by the sadness of loneliness.

The refusal to understand the sufferings of others flows quickly into contempt and tyranny. And these are at the source of all divisions, violence, and hatred. Why have some men power and domination, frequently springing only from the good fortune of birth, whilst others are in misery, powerless, unhappy? Why do those in power despise the powerless? When will they understand that, if they have wealth and power, it is to share with those who have nothing? . . .

Only the Spirit of God can give us the strength to pass from the world of egoism and of acquisition to the world of understanding, of sharing, and of sacrifice: only the Spirit of Love can transform our hearts of stone to hearts of flesh and tender compassion.

My message is a call, a call which finds its source in the eyes of those children I saw in India, in the eyes of the handicapped of

the world, and of all those who are suffering and whose voices
are not heard. May the Spirit of God who loves each one of us
use my poor words to delve into your hearts so that you may
discover the riches of a life given to the service of our fellow men,
so that our world may become a haven of peace — a garden and
not a jungle. May the Spirit of God teach each one of us that
the greatness of life comes not in acquiring, but in dispossessing
and in sharing: not in stifling life, but in giving life.

May God change my heart and yours, giving to each one of
us the courage to become men of peace, prophets of peace. I
mean a peace which is not slumber in satisfaction and wealth,
fearful of wars and revolution, but a sharing in dynamic unity
like a vast and marvelous symphony. In this peace, all men, rich
or poor, black or white, handicapped or not, participate in the
same universal and fraternal love which is but the sign of that
great wedding feast of eternal love and joy to which we are all
convened when our days are finished and when time dies in the
birth of eternity.   — *EH*, 98–99, 102–3

Talk to the Vanier Institute of the Family, 1975

This Institute is doomed to certain death if we make of it an
Institute in defense of traditional family values. I do not need
to tell you that the moment we assume a defensive attitude
we are on the road to dissolution and death. On the level of
ideas, of ideologies, and of life, the best defense is the propagation of truths which attract, which inflame the heart, which
give birth to hope, and which inspire men of good will to vital
and dynamic action....

If we wish to consider the place of the family in our society
as well as an ideal to propose to young people, we must understand the confusion of our youth today, and also its search for
an ideal. If we do not do so, we run the risk of upholding as
a model, a family closed to social values. This well-to-do family, cultivated, correct, and benevolent, with good manners, full

of good will, at times produces professional men with altruistic qualities and charitable well-disposed ladies. This model has perhaps something noble about it, but it is inadequate today. It must be admitted that this model has often been based on a division of humanity between the wealthy and the workers, the whites and the blacks, the cultivated and the ignorant. Too often, there has been terrible pride, strong pharisaism, and intolerant racism....

I would like to go on...to consider the birth of the possessive instinct at the moment of the foundation of a family. I have often been struck by the transformation which reveals itself in the hearts and spirits of the newlyweds. Before marriage, the young man was full of ideals and often acted idealistically. He was ready to struggle in poverty for social justice or for the propagation of philosophical, political, or religious ideas. He could live under difficult conditions. He was generous with his time and possessions. In this spirit, he meets a young woman inspired by the same ideals and they decide to work together. They marry and very quickly they start to install themselves, seeking greater comfort. Their life begins to change radically. Little by little the ideals which had motivated the couple disappear. They tend gradually to close themselves up upon each other and their children. They seek a comfortable family life. If they go out, it is for professional or social reasons. They become imprisoned by their possessions, their way of life and social class, they lose that taste for adventure and that thirst for justice which formerly inspired them. They forget that not very far away, there are grave injustices, the poor, the unfortunate, and the handicapped for whose welfare they had struggled before marriage.

The birth of a child in a family is too often the occasion for withdrawal into its own little world. It should be above all the moment when parents look toward more universal horizons. The appearance of this new person who is free and cannot be led around as one might wish is a true mystery: a mystery which should bring a new depth to the couple and a new gift to the universe....

Parents: you may be disconcerted by the new formulas of the young. But have confidence. Encourage them; do not restrain them. Do not stifle, through money and comfort, the development of the germs of life in them and of an ideal. Let them blossom out in these new forms of poverty. Accept their generosity, which is different from yours. Times have changed....

You, young people, young couples, couples of all ages, who are ready to hear the call, go forward. Follow your conscience. Let your spirits and hearts speak. Do not restrain, or sadden the Spirit. With courage, break through the structures of the past, open your hearts wide to the Spirit of God which is the spirit of welcome and giving, and know that God loves and helps those who follow his Spirit and who live for the unfortunate and who assume real and permanent responsibilities on their behalf. You may have moments of great discouragement, particularly when pressures weigh upon you in order to make you let go. Hold firm to your decision. Your work, often obscure and unrewarding, is the seed that will bring forth the new society of brotherhood, justice, and peace.

— *EH*, 2, 6, 9–10, 19–20

Talk given for the Wit Lectures, Harvard University Divinity School, November 1988

When I was in the navy, I was taught to give orders to others. That came quite naturally to me! All my life I had been taught to climb the ladder, to seek promotion, to compete, to be the best, to win prizes. This is what society teaches us. In doing so we lose community and communion.

But over the years, the people I live with in L'Arche have been teaching and healing me.

They have been teaching me that behind the need for me to win there are my own fears and anguish, the fear of being devalued or pushed aside, the fear of opening up my heart and of being vulnerable or of feeling helpless in the face of others in pain; there is the pain and brokenness of my own heart.

I discovered something which I had never confronted before, that there were immense forces of darkness and hatred within my own heart. At particular moments of fatigue or stress, I saw forces of hate rising up inside me, and the capacity to hurt someone who was weak and was provoking me! That, I think, was what caused me the most pain: to discover who I really am, and to realize that maybe I did not want to know who I really was! I did not want to admit all the garbage inside me. And then I had to decide whether I would just continue to pretend that I was okay and throw myself into hyperactivity, projects where I could forget all the garbage and prove to others how good I was. Elitism is the sickness of us all. We all want to be on the winning team. That is at the heart of apartheid and every form of racism. The important thing is to become conscious of those forces in us and to work at being liberated from them and to discover that the worst enemy is inside our own hearts, not outside!

Yes, the broken and the oppressed have taught me a great deal and have changed me quite radically. They have helped me discover that healing takes place at the bottom of the ladder, not at the top.   —*FBC*, 18–19, 23–24

ECUMENISM AND
INTERFAITH DEVELOPMENT

There are divisions among Christians... but at least we are all united by a fundamental belief in Jesus, in baptism and in the cross. Finding unity with people of different religions is even more difficult: the walls between religions are greater than the walls between churches. Yet we all belong to a common humanity; we are brothers and sisters, born in the image of God, made to know and love God. And so it is obvious that when we welcome a man like Gurunathan, who had been rejected and badly treated for his disabilities, into one of our Indian communities in order to help him grow and find peace, we welcome also his icon of Ganesh, the Hindu god of beginnings, obstacles, of intellect and wisdom. With me and with L'Arche there had to be a renunciation of ideology and an embrace of practicality: what is important to Gurunathan is for him to find out who he is and for us to help him grow more fully as a human person. It's the same when we welcome Muslims and help them attend their local mosque.

Opening doors to other religions involves listening to people and being attentive to their values and their needs. And although there has been a history in the Catholic Church of closing doors, there is also a whole tradition of saints opening doors, and of great, great people — like Mother Teresa and John Paul II — making peace. And of course there are people of other faiths who strive to open doors. Mahatma Gandhi, one of the greatest prophets of the last century, was a man sent by God, a defender of the poorest and the weakest — the "untouchables" — in whom he saw the presence of God. This was a man with a vision of liberation through love, wisdom, and nonviolence; a man who prayed deeply and who said he could do nothing without the strength that comes from prayer; a man who sought to bring men and women of different religions together in peace; a man who encouraged life in community and manual work; a man of God and a man of peace. And I think too of Abdul Ghaffar Khan, a Pashtun political and spiritual leader from what is now Afghanistan, who was a great ally of Gandhi's. He created an "army of peace," and the first vow his followers had to make was to respond to cruelty with forgiveness. He didn't want Afghanistan to choose sides between Hindu India and Muslim Pakistan, but to be open to all religions. For this, he was imprisoned repeatedly by the British and later by the Pakistanis. Throughout his life, he never lost faith in his nonviolent methods or in the compatibility of Islam and nonviolence.   — OLT, 491–93

But L'Arche does not want to be a new church. The document of the International Council (February 1990) on the ecumenical situation of L'Arche today says clearly that L'Arche is called rather to be a source of unity between churches. That is why L'Arche must be linked to the churches. This will cause pain; the experience of division is always painful. Yet, if we want to be credible to our churches, the members of various churches in L'Arche must be true and faithful to their church. That is why we must be centered on our local churches and parishes.

We are called to discover the beauty of living together, being one together as members of different denominations. This does not mean that we try to create a synthesis of all the churches. No. It means that each one is yearning to live the Gospel message and to follow Jesus on the path of love and humility, is rooted in their own church, and gives and reveals to others the charism of their own church. Thus we learn to see how the Holy Spirit is working in others. We begin to appreciate their beliefs and the place from where they come.

The spirituality of L'Arche implies that, called by Jesus, we dare enter into this place of pain, but it is in order to rise again together in the hope and in the reality of unity.   — *PH*, 46

Some people see religion as the root cause of so much wreckage and conflict. My own feeling is that it is not so. At the heart of most, if not all, religions there is a call to become full of the compassion and goodness of God. We need to be grounded in our religion and culture, but also to see that the fulfillment of our culture and our religion is in universal love. In our place of faith and culture, in our church or religious tradition, we are called not only to love all that helps us be open to God and to others, but also to become aware of all that is not God in the way our faith is taught and lived — all that closes us up in ourselves, in our fears and prejudices. Religion can seal us off from others or open us up to them. I am called to listen to your way just as you are called to listen to mine. As we open our hearts to God and to one another, I discover how your way is leading you to truth, to compassion, and to God; you discover how my way is leading me to truth, to compassion, and to God. We gradually become like children, regaining some of our innocence and sincerity and contemplating the beauty of each other and our different ways to God and to peace.

I believe that at the core of many religions there is the desire, force, strength, and compassion to help all people to grow in freedom — to grow to be themselves. Recently the pope brought leaders of all the world religions together at Assisi. They met and talked and prayed. Later they circulated a document, the "Assisi Decalogue of Peace," which embodied the spirit of their meeting: "We commit ourselves to educating people to mutual respect and esteem in order to bring about a peaceful and fraternal coexistence between people of different ethnic groups, cultures, and religions." We see this force too in Mahatma Gandhi, whose great passion was to liberate the most oppressed of people and to help bring mutual respect to Hindus and Muslims. He understood that he could do nothing without God, "sole helper of the helpless." The message of Jesus given in the Gospel of John reveals that it is possible to do good for people, to love them, without possessing them or making them feel inferior. It is possible to bring people together in love.

—*FP,* 34–35

This openness to and respect for others implies a belief
in our common humanity,
in the beauty of other cultures,
and in God's love for each person.
We are one human race.
We human beings are all fundamentally the same.
We are all people with vulnerable hearts,
yearning to love and be loved and valued.

This openness,
which brings together people who are different,
is inspired by love,
a love that sees the value in others

through and in their differences
and the difficulties they might have,
a love that is humble, vulnerable, and welcoming.
Jesus does not enter Jerusalem triumphantly,
but humbly, gently, sitting on a baby donkey.

Peace comes as we approach others humbly, disarmed
from a place of truth,
not from a place of superiority.

Isn't that the vision at the heart of all interdenominational
and interfaith dialogue?   —*DMJ*, 214–15

LOVE YOUR ENEMIES: TRANSFORM HISTORY

The love of one's enemy is at the heart of the Christian message.
Jesus says forcefully, "Love your enemies, do good to those who
hate you, speak well of those who speak badly of you, and pray
for those who abuse you" (Luke 6:27–28).

Jesus' words were spoken in Galilee, near Lake Tiberias. For
many centuries the Jewish people had been overrun by foreign
powers. . . . When we read Jesus' words in such a context an
invitation to love our enemies might seem idealistic or even
sentimental. For the Galileans, Jesus' words could seem like
a provocation, the words of a coward, someone frightened of
violence and confrontation.

But Jesus was neither provocative nor idealistic. He was making a promise of transformation and inner liberation that, if
it had been received, could have transformed the history of
the world.   —*BH*, 146–47

I have had the privilege, through L'Arche and Faith and
Light, to visit many different cultures. While I was in Rwanda
shortly after the genocide, a young woman came up to me and

told me that seventy-five members of her family had been as-
sassinated. She said, "I have so much anger and hate within
me, and I don't know what to do with it. Everybody is talking
about reconciliation, but nobody has asked any forgiveness. I
just don't know what to do with all the hate that is within me."
I said, "I understand. I understand." What more can one say to
a young woman like that who suddenly finds herself all alone
because all her family has been killed? The problem for her was
that she felt guilty because she didn't know how to forgive and
so she was caught up in the world of hate and depression. I
said to her, "Do you know that the first step toward forgiveness is 'no vengeance'? Do you want to kill those who killed
members of your family?" "No," she answered, "there is too
much death." I said, "Well, that is the first step in the process
of forgiveness. The first step."

Forgiveness is a journey; it is not just an event. The first step
in peacemaking is "no vengeance."   — EO, 57

Nonviolence is an attitude when faced with a person, or a group
of people, who are aggressive or who oppress others. It is an attitude where we do not hate or want to use violence, but where
we want the oppressor to change and to grow in justice and
truth. Non-violence is a response to violence, aimed at awakening the oppressor's self-awareness. It is important in all conflict,
and particularly when we feel we must confront an enemy. It
means allowing our own power of aggression to be tempered
with love of those who oppress and with the conviction that
they are not totally bad, that there is good in them and that
they can change. It means desiring life, not death.

Violence as a response to violence is usually the result of fear
arising from our own wounds: we need to defend ourselves, or
to attack, in order to avoid being crushed. Non-violence, mean-
while, is borne out of love. People like Gandhi, Martin Luther
King, Dorothy Day, Jean and Hildegarde Goss-Mayr, and many
others developed not only a spirituality and philosophy of

nonviolence but also the tactics necessary to make nonviolence work in oppressive political and social situations.

— *OJH*, 243

I have not myself had any direct experience of nonviolence as an instrument in political or social affairs. Its success depends upon the mobilization of the media and the support of many people putting pressure on the oppressor. I have, on the other hand, had some experience of nonviolence as a means of easing violence in people, above all in people with handicaps whom we have welcomed to L'Arche from psychiatric hospitals. For some, violence is a cry for attention in the face of oppression and rejection, an attention they need in order to feel that they exist. It springs from anguish and from a broken self-image. It is often a sign of life and hope. If attention is paid to the person in a positive and welcoming way, responding to violence not with violence but with gentleness and understanding, then violence very often disappears....I am not saying that a man intent on killing will always cave in before nonviolence. There are so many different kinds of people with different forms of violence in them. All I know is that if a violent person is treated like a human being rather than a wild animal, there is a chance that he will respond like a human being.   — *OJH*, 244–46

2

" ... with Love ... "

Transformation through Community

*This second chapter, " ...with Love...," explores transfor-
mation through community. This begins with Vanier's own
experience of the transformative power of relationships. The
next sections follow themes crucial to Vanier's particular understanding of the dynamics of shared life: accepting reality; forgiveness and celebration; and practical aspects of living in
community. Over its forty-four-year history, L'Arche has grown
into its own spirituality. Vanier explores communion and covenant with littleness, living the Beatitudes, a spirituality of the
body, of pain, of old age and death, and finally the mission of
people with disabilities.*

VANIER'S EXPERIENCE

In L'Arche I discovered what communion of the heart means.
Before, I used to flee relationships. I was quite austere and or-
ganized my life around studies and prayer. I was frightened of
becoming too vulnerable. I protected myself. I always had to
do things, to know what to do, to control, and to teach. I had
learned how to help others like a superior who knew what to
do in order to make others happy and to put them on the right

path. My heart was open to God but closed to other people as they were, and in their most fundamental needs. It took time for me to learn that you cannot really open your heart to God without opening it to others. John, the beloved disciple of Jesus, says:

> Beloved, let us love one another, since love is from God,
> and everyone who loves is a child of God and knows God.
> Whoever fails to love does not know God
> because God is love.
> Anyone who says, "I love God,"
> and hates his or her brother or sister is a liar,
> since whoever does not love the person
> whom he or she can see
> cannot love God whom he or she has not seen.
> Indeed this is the commandment
> we have received from him [Jesus]
> that whoever loves God, must also love
> his or her brother or sister. (1 John 4:7–8, 20)

Jesus brought me close to people suffering from mental handicaps. They called me to take another path, the path of tenderness, compassion, and communion. They taught me how to celebrate. As I shared my life with them, I discovered the importance of listening and of communicating through nonverbal as well as verbal language. I could not treat them according to my usual norms in working with students who were there to be taught. Raphaël and Philippe and each of the others wanted something else from me: they wanted friendship, which implies understanding. I had to try to listen to their heartbeat, understand their greatest needs, and discover what would help them find meaning in life and hope and trust in themselves. They led me to communion of the heart. However, in order to live this new love and communion faithfully, I needed a new gift of the Holy Spirit.

In L'Arche I was given the gift of the beauty, the gentleness, the purity of heart, and the trust of Raphaël, Philippe, and many others, as well as their pain. The child hidden in their hearts awakened the child within me. There were, of course, moments when I continued to act like the navy officer I had been, and I gave orders. Sometimes that was good and even necessary, but sometimes it was just my need to control, and find security. There was, and still is, a struggle in me, between the need to be right, to control and to have all the answers, and the call to welcome others, simply to be with them, to accept them just as they are, and to have confidence in them and in God. There is still a struggle in me between the need to go up in order to command, and the call to go down, to listen to love, and to be vulnerable with others.

Jesus washing the disciples' feet shows us how God loves and how his disciples, then as now, are called to love and to love "to the very end." The washing of the feet is finally a mystery, like so many of Jesus' acts. We enter into this mystery gradually, through events in which we suffer loss and are stripped more and more of all we possess. When Jesus tells Peter that he will understand "later," Jesus is telling all of his disciples that it is only after a dark night of not knowing, and only through a new gift of the Holy Spirit, that we can penetrate this mystery and live it.

Jesus invites his friends to lay down the garments that give them a special status, to remove the masks that hide their real selves, and to present themselves to others humbly, vulnerably, with all their poverty. To become humble and small requires a loving heart, purified of its fears and human security, ready to love to the end, in order to give life to others.

How does Jesus want us to imitate him? Jesus is asking us to follow him on a path of littleness, forgiveness, trust, communion, and vulnerability without giving up at other moments our role of responsibility where we exercise authority with force and justice, kindness, and firmness. Jesus invites us to live the folly of the Gospel, not to judge others, but to be compassionate, to forgive and to love to the end, even to loving our enemies. This is impossible unless we remove our garments and become poor and naked before God, in order to be more fully "clothed in Christ."   —*SS*, 80–83

Sometimes this littleness is hard to accept. I remember one summer I was responsible for a holiday group from my community. There were fifteen of us. Friends had lent us a house near a Trappist monastery. I loved to get up early to go and pray with the monks. The silence and the peace opened up my heart. Then, around eight o'clock I would walk back down to the house; my heart was a bit heavy. I knew I would have to get some of the people up; they would have dirtied their beds, and I would have to wash and dress them. And then there would be breakfast and so on. All the chores and squabbles of daily life together, all its bodiliness. How far from the peace and quiet of the monastery!

All that inner pain obliged me to go more deeply into the spirituality of L'Arche. It was important for me to find unity in my being, not to have just a deep spirituality early in the morning and then business for the rest of the day. I had to find how to put love and prayerfulness into all my activities and bodily gestures, into all the cleaning and washing up, into all the chores and togetherness of community living.   —*CG*, 301–2

But I ask you to be indulgent if you visit a L'Arche community. Do not be surprised if you find tension, pride, and a lack of sharing and welcoming. Do not be surprised to discover that the ideal L'Arche community does not exist. Each one is made up of people who are struggling, hoping, and growing....

When L'Arche began in 1964, I just wanted to live with a few handicapped people in a Christian spirit. Since then, I have discovered many new dimensions of L'Arche. I have discovered that to live with the poor and the weak is very demanding, precisely because they are asking me to change, to grow, and to be more compassionate and wise. I have learned how much I must die to my own ideas and to myself in order to listen to them and live with them. I have learned about the need for precision and firmness so that we can all grow. I have discovered how difficult it is for assistants to put down roots. I have learned about L'Arche in developing countries and how much we must respect and love other cultures and how easily we judge and impose our ways. I have discovered the importance of integration into neighborhoods and the importance of co-operation with families. Above all, I have discovered how handicapped people can be a source of peace and unity in our terribly divided world, provided we are willing to listen to them, to follow them and to share our lives with them.   — *CLA*, 8–9

We need to touch the truth of who we are.
It is then, as we grow gradually
into the acceptance of our wounds and fragility,
that we grow into wholeness,
and from that wholeness, life begins to flow forth
to others around us.

It is important to take time to be silent,
to be alone with Jesus,
to look at the reality of who we are,
be in contact with our hidden places of pain
and little by little we can become a friend of our weakness.

In 1980, when I left the role of community leader in Trosly,
I lived a year at La Forestière, one of our homes
for ten men and women with profound disabilities.
I have told you about Eric, but there was also Lucien.
Lucien was born with severe mental and physical disabilities.
He cannot talk or walk or move his arms.
His body is a bit twisted
and he has to remain in his wheelchair or in his bed.
He never looks anyone directly in the eyes.
Lucien's father died when he was twelve.
He lived the first thirty years of his life with his mother,
who cared for him and understood Lucien and his needs;
she could interpret all his body language.

He was at peace and felt secure with her.
One day she fell sick and had to go to the hospital.
Lucien was put into another hospital
and was plunged into a totally strange and unknown world.
He had lost all his familiar points of reference;
no one seemed to understand him.
Screams of anguish rose up in him
which were unbearable to hear.
Finally he came to La Forestière.
We felt quite powerless in the face of his constant
        screaming.
If we tried to touch him to calm him down,
this very touch seemed to increase his anguish.
There was nothing to do but to wait.

The pitch of Lucien's scream was piercing
and seemed to penetrate the very core of my being,
awakening my own inner anguish.
I could sense anger, violence, and even hatred
rising up within me.
I would have been capable of hurting him to keep him quiet.
It was as if a part of my being that I had learned to control
was exploding.
It was not only Lucien's anguish
that was difficult for me to accept
but the revelation of what was inside my own heart,
 — my capacity to hurt others —
I who had been called to share my life with the weak,
had a power of hatred for a weak person! . . .

How painful it is for us to look reality in the face,
to discover our own fragility
and our capacity for anger and hatred.
The temptation to avoid or run away from
those who reveal our inner limits and brokenness is so great.
The roots of much racism, rejection, and exclusion are here.

It is important not to run away,
but to find someone with whom we can speak
about these shadow areas of our being,
these inner "demons," the "wolf" within us,
someone who can help us not to be controlled by them
so that they no longer haunt our lives.   — *BTS*, 61–63

REALITY

I have always wanted to write a book called "The Right to be a Rotter." A fairer title is perhaps "The Right to be Oneself."

One of the great difficulties of community life is that we sometimes force people to be what they are not: we stick an ideal image on them to which they are obliged to conform. We then expect too much of them and are quick to judge or to label. If they don't manage to live up to this image or ideal, then they become afraid they won't be loved or that they will disappoint others. So they feel obliged to hide behind a mask. Sometimes they succeed in living up to the image; they are able to follow all the rules of community. Superficially this may give them a feeling of being perfect, but this is an illusion.

In any case, community is not about perfect people. It is about people who are bonded to each other, each of whom is a mixture of good and bad, darkness and light, love and hate. And community is the only earth in which each can grow without fear toward the liberation of the forces of love which are hidden in them. But there can be growth only if we recognize the potential, and this will never unfold if we prevent people from discovering and accepting themselves as they are, with their gifts and their wounds. They have the right to be rotters, to have their own dark places, and corners of envy and even hatred in their hearts. These jealousies and insecurities are part of our wounded nature. That is our reality.   — *CG*, 42–43

There is before us the ideal presented by Jesus, which is a great ideal, and at the same time we try to accept the reality that we are terribly weak and unable to reach the ideal.

Not only are we weak, but we are continually hiding our own weakness. In our civilization we cannot say we are weak. If one admits to weakness, he admits death. We have a need to be right, to be conscious of our capacity and even more to convince others of our capacity, and to prove that we are someone.

One day a professor from the Sorbonne came to dinner with us, and we were trying to guess the population of a certain French town. Everyone threw in an idea — from fifty million people to five hundred. The professor was terribly embarrassed because he had to be right: so he asked what year we wanted the population for and discussed the movement of industry and so on, over five whole minutes. And in the end he didn't win. But he couldn't bear the thought of losing to all these people who were mentally handicapped—he, a professor of the Sorbonne!

It is difficult to accept that we make mistakes. When for example, we as cook burn something, we become angry or we find it difficult to accept, whereas in reality, the cook should be allowed to burn things from time to time. Instead of being able to say simply, "Well, today I'm not a good cook," we cut ourselves off from other people. The fact is, maybe we aren't very good cooks, but we can take the cookbook and grow in cooking.

We must try to look at reality, the reality of our own weakness and then allow each other to make mistakes, trying with the help of the Spirit to accept each other.   —BSL, 1–5

One of the best qualities of the men and women I live with is that they live for the present. They have sufferings in their past and they have aspirations for the future, but because they are people whose hearts are more developed than their minds, they have the capacity to live in the reality of the present.

We have had some wonderful pilgrimages together. Once in Portugal, our bus started billowing smoke from the wheels. This seemed a bit odd, so we limped into a town, and as we didn't have money for hotels, we went and knocked on the door of the priest. We trooped into his office and sat down, and when he came in and saw our motley crew his eyes popped out of his head. We were just singing and praying, completely abandoned to what might happen. I asked if he could find us somewhere to stay for the night, and although I think he was quite keen to get rid of us, he was very kind. He put us in a big dormitory but didn't manage to find us any dinner. So there we were, about fifteen of us, in this hot room, with about three plums and a bit of stale bread each, and some tepid water. We asked each of our men what they wanted to drink, and when they said orangeade, that's what they got, even though it was really only the tepid water. So we had everything you can think of — champagne, burgundy, lemonade. It was really beautiful, the way each person lived the reality of the tepid water!

On the way back, I was driving the bus when suddenly there was a great explosion — the windshield had shattered. I couldn't see a thing, but was trying to avoid a car I'd seen coming the other way before the bang and keep out of the ditch at the same time. In the middle of all this, Dede said, "Isn't it beautiful! The windshield looks just like crystal." That's living in the present moment; that's seeing the beauty of reality!

In all things, wherever we may be, we must learn to welcome the reality and the people the moment brings us. . . . This is the now, and this is where we must learn to live.

— *BNA*, 138–39

The pain Jesus confronts is that
while some are brought to faith by miracles,
others harden their hearts in the face of such a challenge
to their sense of reality.
They do not want to see; they are blind to reality;
they cannot believe that if Jesus is really from God,
then God will look after them
as God has done so often in the past.

Why do they refuse to trust Jesus?
Is it their fear of an uprising
and the retaliation of the Romans?
Is it their fear of change?
Is it their fear of losing power and control of the situation?
Is it their fear of trusting and surrendering to God?
Is it jealousy of Jesus, because so many are going to him?
It is probably a mixture of all these things,
which find a home in the dark areas of our own hearts.
We, too, can refuse to look at and listen humbly to reality,
to read the signs of the Holy Spirit
in what is going on in the world and in the church around us.
We can also refuse to trust the power of God
within us and in others.

Jesus calls each one of us to rise up.

There are different levels of understanding
in the Gospel of John.
There is the historical level:
the fact that a man who had been dead for four days
comes back to life,
a miracle that proclaims
the glory, majesty, and power of God, Lord of life and death.
The crowd sees this glory and many believe.

There is also a symbolic level. Aren't we all Lazarus?
Are there not parts in each one of us that are dead,
caught up in a culture of death?
All that is dead in us,
more or less hidden in our unconscious self,
in the shadow areas or the "tomb" of our being,
provokes a kind of death around us.
We judge and condemn and push people down,
wanting to show that we are better than they.
We refuse to listen to those who are different,
and so we hurt them.

All these destructive acts have their origin
in all that is dead within us,
all that creates a stench in the hidden parts of our being,
which we do not want to look at or admit.

Jesus wants us to rise up and to become fully alive.
He calls us out of the tomb we carry within us,
just as God called Ezekiel to raise up from the dead
all those people of Israel
who were lying in the tomb of despair:
    Thus says the Lord God,
    "I am going to open your tombs
    and raise you up from your tombs, O my people....
    I will put my spirit in you and you shall live."
                                              (Ezek. 37:12, 14)

This is what Jesus wants for each one of us today.
                                              —*DMJ*, 202–4

The first principle in accompaniment is to help the other person
to live in reality and not in dreams, theories, and illusions, to accept who he or she really is, with their inner handicaps, wounds
and shadow areas, so that they do not live in a constant state of
frustration, guilt, and stress. There is no need to be perfect. Of
course, we need hope, and a vision for the future, but these are
very different from illusions and dreams that have no basis in
reality, that are the fruit of an imagination, cut off from reality.
                                              —*OJH*, 156–57

Happiness is accepting and choosing life, not just submitting
grudgingly to it. It comes when we choose to be who we are,
to be ourselves, at this present moment of our lives; we choose
life as it is, with all its joys, pain, and conflicts. Happiness is
living and seeking the truth, together with others in community, and assuming responsibility for our lives and the lives of
others. It is accepting the fact that we are not infinite, but can
enter into a personal relationship with the Infinite, discovering

the universal truth and justice that transcends all cultures: each person is unique and sacred. We are not just seeking to be what others want us to be or to conform to the expectations of family, friends, or local ways of being. We have chosen to be who we are, with all that is beautiful and broken in us. We do not slip away from life and live in a world of illusions, dreams, or nightmares. We become present to reality and to life so that we are free to live according to our personal conscience, our sacred sanctuary, where love resides within us and we see others as they are in the depth of their being. We are not letting the light of life within us be crushed, and we are not crushing it in others. On the contrary, all we want is for the light of others to shine.   —FP, 54–55

FORGIVENESS AND CELEBRATION

Community is the place of forgiveness. In spite of all the trust we may have in each other, there are always words that wound, self-promoting attitudes, situations where susceptibilities clash. That is why living together implies a cross, a constant effort, an acceptance which is daily, and mutual forgiveness.

Too many people come into community to find something, to belong to a dynamic group, to discover a life which approaches the ideal. If we come into community without knowing that the reason we come is to learn to forgive and be forgiven seven times seventy-seven times, we will soon be disappointed.

But forgiveness is not simply saying to someone who has had a fit of anger, slammed the doors, and behaved in an anti-social or "anti-community" way, "I forgive you." When people have power and are well settled in community, it is easy to "wield" forgiveness.

To forgive is also to understand the cry behind the behavior. People are saying something through their anger and/or anti-social behavior. Perhaps they feel rejected. Perhaps they feel that no one is listening to what they have to say or maybe they feel incapable of expressing what is inside them. Perhaps the community is being too rigid or too legalistic and set in its ways; there may even be a lack of love and of truth. To forgive is also to look into oneself and to see where one should change, where one should also ask for forgiveness and make amends.

To forgive is to recognize once again — after separation — the covenant which binds us together with those we do not get along with well; it is to be open and listening to them once again. It is to give them space in our hearts. That is why it is never easy to forgive. We too must change. We must learn to forgive and forgive and forgive every day, day after day. We need the power of the Holy Spirit in order to open up like that.
— *CG*, 37–38

Community is difficult. There are people who trigger off pain inside us. Some people remind us of unhappy childhood experiences. Some people, by the way they speak and by their attitude, trigger off fears and pain inside of us. These people are the enemy. They block us and prevent us from flowering. They reveal to us our pain and our brokenness. But such enemies can also become the healers, precisely because they reveal to us how broken we are. They reveal to us something about the truth of ourselves, and we would rather run away from the truth.

The enemy reveals that there is something horrible inside of us, a whole world of inner pain that can stir us to hate. The enemy is the one who will teach us the most important lesson about human existence: how to forgive ourselves and others, how to resolve conflicts, how to live in peace with one another, how to accept differences, and how to accept ourselves. And as we accept ourselves, we enter into the paths of forgiveness and wholeness.   — *ILWH*, 104

Forgiveness and celebration are at the heart of community. These are the two faces of love. Celebration is a communal experience of joy, a song of thanksgiving. We celebrate the fact of being together; we give thanks for the gifts we have been given. Celebration nourishes us, restores hope, and brings us the strength to live with the suffering and difficulties of everyday life.   — CG, 313

There is a link between forgiveness and celebration. True celebration implies forgiveness and flows from it. When the prodigal son returned home after a debauched life, the father forgave him and gathered everyone together for a feast. He said to his servants: "Hurry up! Bring the most beautiful robe and put it on him. Place a ring on his finger and shoes on his feet. Bring the fatted calf, kill it, we will eat and celebrate because my son who was dead has returned to life. He was lost and he is found! Let us celebrate!" (Luke 15:22–24).

Some people would like community celebrations to be spontaneous; they say they can celebrate only if they feel like it. However, if we waited until everyone spontaneously felt like celebrating, there would not be very many celebrations! Between a rigid ritual and a spontaneous manifestation, there is a middle road. Celebrations need to be prepared. It is important to plan the songs and the order of the various activities, but at the same time remaining flexible and able to change: to prolong certain moments of fun, joy, grace and times of silence, or to cut things short if necessary. It is often the unexpected and the spontaneous which nourish most.

Many of those with disabilities need to be stimulated and called into activities. This can require energy. It could be so much easier just to put them in front of the television, or a show that others perform, or simply let them do their own thing. Once they are called to the celebration, they become the heart of it, and draw others into it, creating a warmth and special joy.
                                      — MW, 178–79

Food is important, and it should be good. Meals shouldn't be just something slopped onto the table; they should be times of communion. This is hard to convey in North America, where meals are often just something you throw into your stomach

and have to get through. Certainly Canadians often find meals
at L'Arche really long. And they are. But the meal is a whole
ritual which begins with the soup and goes right through to the
washing up. Washing up is an important time, because people
work together, just as they share and communicate during the
meal itself.

Meals are sharing, so it's important that the food should be
shared too. Nowadays there's a tendency for everyone to have
their own little pat of butter, their own little bottle of Coca-
Cola, their own little packet of salt and pepper. One bottle for
everyone to share may be less hygienic and less efficient, but it
will bring more friendship. Even if you can find nothing else to
say to someone, you can at least ask him for the salt, and this
is the beginning of communication.

Meals shouldn't be serious times. They are times for laughter,
because laughter opens people up, and a group that laughs is a
group that is relaxed. And when people are relaxed, they can
begin to grow together. Relaxation is like good soil, in which
love can begin to grow. Nothing grows in hard soil. This is why
it is important to have good food and good wine — in France
at least. You may have people who squabble over the liturgy or
theological problems, but at least let them relax over the food
and wine and avoid ulcers!

Try to play stupid games — any sort. Let us come like children, to laugh and enjoy ourselves. This is what a community
should learn to do — to relax and to welcome people. And as it
grows, it learns to know people, with their needs, their hopes,
and their aspirations. Then it begins to accept, not judging or
wanting people other than they are, but gradually discovering
the music of their beings.   — BNA, 82–83

Celebration and communication through joy are particularly
important for men and women who have grown up with the
sense that they are a disappointment to their parents. Celebration reveals to them the joy of being together. Through

celebration we can say to them, "We rejoice that you exist, just as you are."

Celebration creates unity in the community, and also flows from it. When a business is particularly successful, or a team wins at some sport, or someone is promoted, there are prizes and applause and honors. The winners are regarded as the best and the strongest. But celebration springs not from the fact that someone has won or proved him or herself to be the strongest, but from the fact that the members of a community love each other, are happy to be together, each taking his or her place. Celebration flows from the union of hearts and from mutual trust.

A community that does not celebrate is in danger of becoming just a group of people that gets things done.   —*OJH*, 199

True belly laughs are important in community life. When a group laughs in this way, many pains are swept away.

—*CG*, 316

LIVING IN COMMUNITY

Community is one of the most beautiful realities — brothers and sisters loving and being together. It is also one of the most difficult to accomplish.

Living together is difficult for human beings. Goldfish seem to manage it — you rarely see head-on collisions. Cows seem to manage all right in the same pasture — at least until the bull comes along. But put ten men together in a house and very quickly you have a hotel. Put ten women together and you soon have problems, though these are nothing to the problems you get when you put five men and five women together.

Once together, we very quickly start to squabble. We each want more than the others. We get aggressive because one of our number irritates us. Tensions arise, and then everyone starts to be very polite to hide their fear of those tensions. You can sense the coldness as people slide down corridors not daring to look at each other for fear of an explosion, or bury their head in a book when another goes past.

Yet as soon as you go into some homes you can sense a peace, an openness, a welcome, in the meeting of eyes and the smile that communicates without words.

Few people seem to know the laws of community.

Community takes a long time to form. It takes a long time for barriers to drop, for mutual confidence to grow, for nonverbal communication to become more important than words. A community is only a community when most of the people in it have made the passage from "the community for me" to "me for the community." A community is only a community when most of the people in it are conscientiously trying to seek the fulfillment, peace, and happiness of every other member of it.

— *BNA,* 78

People who have lived alone normally find their first month in community a great joy. Everyone around them seems to be a saint; everyone seems so happy. Then in the second month, everyone is a devil. Everyone has mixed motives for whatever he does. Everyone is something of a hypocrite. Everyone is so greedy that he takes just the piece of meat I had my eye on. They talk when I want to be silent and when I want to talk they cut me off with their long silent looks. It's a conspiracy.

In the third month, they are neither saints nor devils. They are people who have come together to strive and to love. They are neither perfect nor imperfect, but like everyone else a mixture of the two. They are people who are growing, and that means the good is in the growth and the bad is what prevents growth.

This is reality. We are people who have come together to share our poverty, our hopes, our aspirations, and our desires to grow in the Spirit. We must move quickly into accepting this reality, into accepting that all of us are wounded by sin and by egoism. Unfortunately, the second "month"— this time element

is of course just a symbol and this can take ten years to arrive —
is too much for many people and they run away.

We must accept that the growth from egoism to love, from
community for myself to myself for community, is a long and
sometimes a hard road, paved with joys and sufferings. It begins
simply.

It begins by accepting our differences, and by beginning to
know one another. What brings this member of the community
peace? What hurts him? What brings him out of or plunges him
into depression? What calms him, what irritates him? All this is
important when you are living with someone. You must know
what will help him to be at peace and to live in the spirit of love.

Some people need to be left alone when they are in depression. Don't go up to them and start pawing them, because they
might explode. Others need attention; they need a cup of tea, to
be drawn into conversation, a word of gentleness.

You can know who needs which only when you have lived
with them for some time. It takes time to know their needs,
their call, their thirst. It takes time to know the little things that
can hurt them.   — BNA, 80–81

There are two enemies of community for us: those people we
call our enemies and those we call our "friends."

The enemy is the one who rubs me the wrong way, the one
I disagree with, the one I criticize or who criticizes me. Our
enmity can be theological or even liturgical — there are more
battles over liturgy than you would think possible. The enemy is
the one who annoys me because his background or language is
not the same as mine. He is the one who is always complaining
that the soup is too hot or too cold. He is the one who always
wants exactly the television program that I do not. The enemy
is the one I cut off, the one who ceases to exist for me, and he
can be found in every home and every community.

This is to be expected, because God does not call together
groups of people who are naturally adapted to one another. He
calls people who are very different in their origins, customs, and

ways of thinking and he asks them to live together because they believe in Jesus Christ. Yet enmity brings destruction of community, for where there is enmity there are factions. Community means that most of the people are seeking to love and to find the fulfillment of every other person in that community, whatever their origins, liturgical preferences, or favorite television programs.

The other enemy of community can be human friendship and sympathy. It brings destruction if it means the grouping together of people of the same background and aspirations to close themselves off from other members of the community. It brings destruction if it does not open the group to all the other members of the community.   — BNA, 79

Using our gifts is building community. If we are not faithful to our gifts, we are harming the community and each of its members as well. So it is important that all members know what their gifts are, use them and take responsibility for developing them; it is important that the gift of each member is recognized and that each is accountable to the others for the use to which this gift is put. We all need each other's gifts; we must encourage their growth and our fidelity to them. Everyone will find their place in community according to their gift. They will become not only useful but unique and necessary to the others. And so rivalry and jealousy will evaporate.   — CG, 50

In L'Arche, people with mental handicaps live together with "assistants," people who want to share their lives with them and become their friends. We live in small houses, well integrated into a village or a city neighborhood. People who are weak and fragile obviously need the help of those who are stronger. In L'Arche, however, we are discovering that the opposite is equally true: people who are stronger need those who are more fragile. We need one another.

People who are powerless and vulnerable attract what is most beautiful and most luminous in those who are stronger:

they call them to be compassionate, to love intelligently, and not only in a sentimental way. Those who are weak help those who are more capable to discover their humanity and to leave the world of competition in order to put their energies at the service of love, justice, and peace. The weak teach the strong to accept and integrate the weakness and brokenness of their own lives, which they often hide behind masks.

A few years ago we welcomed Loic into one of our homes in Trosly-Breuil (France). Today Loic is forty years old, but he looks like a child of five. He is small, weak, cannot talk, and is limited in his capacity to understand. But Loic has a sensitive, loving heart; he senses immediately whether or not the person next to him is open, attentive, and loving. I lived for a year in his house, La Forestière, and, though we live in different houses today, we still remain close. Loic taught me to be more attentive and loving; he opened my heart and the intelligence of my heart. Even though I can still encounter today the temptations to seek success and recognition, he brought down many of my defense mechanisms and my need always to have the last word.

People who are weak and vulnerable can also awaken in us what is most dark and ugly. Their cry, their provocations, their constant demands, and their depression can unmask our own anguish and violence. But isn't it true that in order to grow in our humanity, we need to recognize the violence and the power of hatred within our own heart, all that we consider shameful and try to hide? In L'Arche, we are gradually learning how to manage these fears and energies in a positive way and how to free ourselves from the powers of destruction within us.

— SS, 2–3

Six years ago, in our community in France, we welcomed Antonio, a small man of twenty-six who has a severe learning disability and is fragile in many ways. Constantly in need of oxygen, he cannot walk or speak or fend for himself. He lives in one of our homes with five other people with severe handicaps and five assistants. If you approach him and call him by his name, he responds with a big smile and shining eyes. There is no depression, no revolt, no anger in him. He is transparent with trust. Assistants living with him tell me often that Antonio has transformed their lives. He is leading them from a world of conflict, competition, and hierarchy into a world of tenderness, healing, and covenantal relationships.

The folly of the Gospel is the folly of the Word who became flesh. He became a child, became weakness, in order to bring together in unity all of God's children. The folly of the Gospel is the presence of Jesus hidden in the weak and the powerless in order to open and heal the hearts of the powerful and the rich. Jesus says:

> Whoever welcomes one of these little ones in my name, welcomes me, and whoever welcomes me, welcomes the one who sent me. (Matt. 12:5)

This remains one of the most mysterious and challenging promises of Jesus.

In community with the poor, everything is not simple and gentle. To respond to the cry and the needs of Antonio implies loss. Antonio heals, but at the same time, he disturbs, because his needs are great. He disturbs also because living with Antonio, everything seems so useless, little, physical, and emotional. Nothing big, nothing great. Giving baths, cleaning, cooking, eating, laughing, getting angry, praying. For many assistants, it can be a good experience, an awakening, but it is not easy for them to put down roots with Antonio and others like him who have been crushed by sickness, weakness, and rejection. What is the meaning of all this?

...We are not all like Antonio, who seems to accept so beautifully his brokenness. A light of peace and the warmth of tenderness arise from all that is shattered and broken in him. Others cry out in their pain, their revolt, and their anguish. This awakens the pain, the darkness, the fears, and the wounds in me and in others. They reveal not only the beauty but also the violence of my own heart, my capacity to hate and to kill. But this too can be a healing experience, if we accept it and find its fullest meaning.   — *RFP*, 133–35

THE SPECIFIC SPIRITUALITY
OF L'ARCHE

The spirituality of L'Arche is to descend the ladder of human promotion to be with the weak and the poor, to build family and community with them, to serve them. It is not just to do things for them, but to befriend them, to live simply with them.

The spirituality of L'Arche is specified in a clear way when Jesus says:

> When you give dinner or a supper, do not invite your friends nor your brothers and sisters or relatives nor your rich neighbors lest they also invite you in return and you be repaid. But when you give a banquet, invite poor people, the maimed, the lame and the blind, and you shall be blessed, because they cannot repay you. Your recompense will be in the resurrection of the just.
>
> (Luke 14:12–14)

In the biblical vision, to eat together means to become friends, to enter a covenant, to be bonded together as brothers and sisters.

In L'Arche assistants are not there essentially to do things for people with disabilities but rather to become their friends, their brothers and sisters. We are bonded together in a covenant of love; we are of the same family. This does not exclude, of course, our doing things for them nor that we be competent in teaching skills and in our care for them, nor that we know how to dialogue verbally with those who are able to receive and appreciate such communication. But it is to say that what is specific in L'Arche is the covenant of love that binds us all together.

This bonding implies eating together and such realities as presence, communion, and touch. It means there is communication of the heart through our bodies. There is a whole new mode of communicating through the way we touch and look and laugh, the way we listen, the way we are present to others. This is most evident with those who have severe disabilities, who cannot talk or walk, but it is true with all our people. They are more sensitive to body language than to verbal language, though both are necessary.   —PH, 16–17

To love someone does not mean first of all to do things for that person; it means helping her to discover her own beauty, uniqueness, the light hidden in her heart and the meaning of her life. Through love a new hope is communicated to that person and thus a desire to live and to grow. This communication of love may require words, but love is essentially communicated through nonverbal means: our attitudes, our eyes, our gestures, and our smiles. This is the whole pedagogy of L'Arche, which we try to put into practice in spite of all our inadequacies. —SS, 5

I must admit that L'Arche was badly founded. When I began with Père Thomas, neither of us knew what L'Arche was about. As I started to live with Raphaël and Philippe I began little by little to discover what it was. The first communities were not guided very much. Seeds were thrown into the ground, and they grew without knowledgeable gardeners.

Over the years we have all learned a bit more about what L'Arche is. It is something totally new. There are still many unanswered questions. Together we are trying to answer them. But when one question is answered, many others spring up that await answers! . . .

The spirituality of L'Arche implies that we act like rabbits and not like giraffes. Giraffes see from afar where they should go. Rabbits sniff their way. We are sniffing our way along, and we will go in the right direction if we keep eating with the poor, living with them, listening to them.   —PH, 47–48

Certainly, all of our communities would love to have stability, a large group of well trained people, ardent in spirituality, focused in a prayerful life, recognized and valued by local authorities, convinced of the vision of the weak, who will heal the strong, secure financially, and so on, and so on.

The reality is not like that. Our communities are pilgrim communities. We are not even sure who are or are not members of our communities, because membership is more of a spirit than a law. We never have enough assistants, so few are prepared to stay a long time in our homes. We have a beautiful vision, a vision to be like the yeast in the bread of society, and where the weak heal the strong. We are continually shaken by unexpected events, strong winds which make people topple over, but also extraordinary events when we can almost see the long hand of God protecting us and holding those who are the weakest and the most vulnerable.

L'Arche and Faith and Light are not like well-constructed, well-known monuments, glorious cathedrals, prestigious universities, efficient hospitals — all fixed, stable, on firm ground. We are but little homes filled with happy prayerful celebrating people whose fragility is marked on their bodies, minds, and spirits, and with assistants and friends who believe in a spirit of love and of tenderness. Yes we are a pilgrim people, holding a vision and walking daily to a promised land of love. However, let's face it, there are many cultural and historic factors in our modern world which render difficult the living out of the vision. Yet L'Arche and Faith and Light are born of God, and God will watch over us.

— Letter from Jean Vanier, May 2008 (unpublished)

Living the Beatitudes

The Beatitudes are at the heart of Jesus' message. They are the foundation of all his teaching and the charter for all Christians. At the same time, the Beatitudes are a gift of God. They put people into a new relationship with God. In the Gospels,

there are the well-known "official" Beatitudes in Matthew and
Luke, but there are other, more hidden Beatitudes throughout
the Gospels....

Blessed are those who eat with the poor (Luke 14); blessed
are those who believe without seeing (John 20:29); blessed are
those who listen to the word of God and put it into practice
(Luke 11:28).... And then there is the blessedness of washing
each other's feet.

In the original Jerusalem Bible, the Greek word for "beatitude" was translated by "happy." That is not wrong, if we
understand the deepest meaning of happiness. For it is truly a
joy to wash the feet of the poor and weak, to live in communion with them. There is a deep but often hidden joy in being
united to Jesus in his pain, tears, and rejection; to know that he
is with us in it all. There is also an inner joy in discovering the
meaning of all our suffering.   — SS, 27–28

The Bible is the history of these two worlds and of these two
enemies, Lazarus and the rich man. Jesus put himself between
these two worlds. He saw and identified with the world of the
rejected, the humble, and the little. He said, "Come, Live!"
He came to give light to the blind, pardon to sinners, and to
announce a time of grace and forgiveness. He announced his
message by calling all men to follow him and to take their place
between these two worlds.

> Blessed are you in your poverty; you are not shut in the false
>   world of convention, riches, and human security.
> Blessed are you because you are gentle; you refuse violence
>   and aggressiveness; you allow yourself to be led by the
>   Spirit into the world of tenderness and patience.
> Blessed are you because you hunger and thirst for justice;
>   your heart beats in the rhythm of the heart of Jesus.
> Blessed are you because your heart is pure; you do not accept
>   compromises.

> Blessed are you because you are merciful; you attach your
> heart to misery; you will receive mercy and no one will
> see your sin.
> Blessed are you because at all times and at every moment
> you want to be an instrument of peace; seeking unity,
> understanding, and reconciliation above all things.
> Blessed are you because you have allowed your own con-
> science to develop; you have not been swayed by what
> people might say about you and you have acted as
> a free individual; you have accepted persecution; you
> have not been afraid to proclaim the truth.

Then Jesus turned to the world of the self-satisfied and declared,

> Woe to you that are rich...that are full now...that laugh
> now, for you shall mourn and weep. (Luke 6:24)

> It is easier for a camel to go through the eye of a needle than
> for a rich man to enter the kingdom of God.
> (Luke 18:25)

The rich man is rich precisely because he does not know how
to give, because he does not know how to share. If he had
known how to share he wouldn't be rich any longer. He who
has shut himself into a world of defensiveness and pride cannot enter into the kingdom of sharing. The key to the kingdom,
the only key, is openness: to open one's arms, one's eyes, one's
heart, because the kingdom of God is just like that — the place
of meeting, of communion, of peace, and of giving.

—BNA, 21–22

The spirit of L'Arche is based on the Gospels, the good news of
Jesus Christ. The Beatitudes are at the heart of our communities. If we forget this initial inspiration, then the real meaning
of the handicapped people will be lost; they will no longer be
seen in their capacity to live and grow in their openness to God
and in the beauty hidden in their weakness; assistants will refuse
to enter into a covenant with them. They will tend to use the

Now, through this intimate action, he affirms a personal relationship with each one. As he knelt down, he must have looked at each one with such gentleness and love, calling him by name. At the same time this gesture is a "good-bye." Jesus knows that the next day he will be put to death; this is the last time he will touch his friends. He must have touched the feet of each one so gently, with such affection, with all the fire of the love and the humility that unite him to his Father.

Being so vulnerable and sensitive, Jesus perhaps had to do this not only to express his love, but to communicate the communion that he has with his Father, and that he yearns to live with his disciples.

Even though the disciples do not understand, and Peter's reticence is proof of their lack of understanding, each one lets Jesus wash his feet. Each permits Jesus' love to become communion, in other words, for love to be given and received, for love to be shared. To remove one's shoes before another person already expresses a certain intimacy with that person, doesn't it? Isn't that the meaning of God's words to Moses: "Take off your shoes, for the ground you are standing on is holy ground" (Exod. 3:5)? With the Word becoming flesh, the new "holy ground" is the body of Jesus. Through the gift of the Holy Spirit, each person's body becomes "holy ground," the new temple of God.

The way Jesus touched his disciples must have made them understand, even if only later, the sacredness of their own bodies. The body is the place where the Father dwells.

The friendship and relationship contained in washing feet, the way it communicates love, were revealed to me in a special way when I lived my sabbatical year in La Forestière, one of our L'Arche homes that welcomes ten men and women with severe handicaps. None of these people can speak and most cannot walk or eat by themselves. Each one has felt abandoned. What is important is to reveal to them their value and beauty, to help transform the negative image they have of themselves into a positive one and to communicate to them a desire to live.

This communication is essentially through touch, presence, and a nonverbal language. One of the most meaningful moments of the day in La Forestière is bath time, a time of relationship, when by the way we touch and bathe each person we can help each one become aware of his or her own beauty and value. Words are, of course, absolutely vital in some situations as they explain what is being done and affirm the meaning of certain actions, but the gesture itself is of vital importance.

When love is given and received, a trust and peace enter the heart, which the face and the whole body radiate. A few years ago Peter arrived in L'Arche. He was quite a difficult man who absolutely refused to communicate with anyone. He was completely closed up in himself with delinquent tendencies. One day we discovered that he had athlete's foot. The doctor prescribed some medication and asked us to wash his feet three times a day. From the day we started to touch and bathe his feet Peter began to open up. His whole attitude toward us changed. This showed us once again the importance of the washing of the feet.

While I was living at La Forestière, I became more aware of the importance of Paul's words: "Do you not realize that you are a temple of the Holy Spirit, who is in you and whom you received from God in you? ...So use your body for the glory of God" (1 Cor. 6:19).

If the body is truly the dwelling place of God, a holy ground, then all our relationships are transformed. When we meet and touch others, we do so with even more respect as we realize their life is holy. When Jesus washes his disciples' feet and asks us to do the same, is he not showing us the importance of meeting each other, touching each other, with simplicity, gentleness, and great respect, because each person is precious?

—*SS*, 35–38

John Paul II was another person who came to truly understand L'Arche, but perhaps only when he became ill with Parkinson's disease. I remember the first time I had breakfast with him (in 1987, when he was still well) and I explained to him how a

disabled person, like Eric, who was blind and deaf, was a healing presence in L'Arche. In his littleness Eric transformed those
who lived a relationship with him. John Paul said to somebody
afterward that he hadn't understood what I meant. It's after
he became sick that a deep bond arose between us, when he
understood how someone "made little" by a severe handicap
could transform others. In January 2004, at a meeting in Rome
that focused on the disabled, John Paul said that people with
disabilities can help us to discover a new world where love is
stronger than aggressiveness. After the meeting, I called his sec-
retary to ask if I could attend the Pope's Mass; he said yes but
that I would be alone with John Paul. It was a very special,
moving time together — a time of prayer, communion, and mutual recognition. He knew that I loved him in his weakness and
I knew that he loved L'Arche and me in our weaknesses too.

— OLT, 548–49

Founded on Pain

We must not be idealistic about people with mental handicaps.
Some have been victims of so much contempt and violence,
which they have stored up inside themselves, that there can be
an explosion of violence, especially when they first come to live
in a L'Arche community. Anger and depression remain with certain people with a mental handicap for the whole of their lives.
At L'Arche, there are moments of elation, but there are also
moments of great pain and anguish.

But for the people living with them, there is a positive side
to these difficulties. They reveal our limitations, our vulnerabil-
ities, our need to be reassured and understood, our blindness,
our blockages, all those things that we hid from ourselves and
from others before coming to L'Arche. When you live a life of
fairly intense relationships, in a community, you quickly discover who you are. It is impossible to hide anything. If in every
person's heart there is a thirst for communion and friendship,

there are also deep wounds, fears, and a whole world of darkness that govern our lives in a hidden way. Coming to know this shadow side, and then to accept it, seems to me to be a first step toward true self-knowledge.   — *OJH*, xii–xiii

I am not ignoring the importance of celebrations in L'Arche and Faith and Light or all the joys of communion between us, and I do not want to be pessimistic. But the experience of these thirty-four years in L'Arche have shown me that in order to be faithful on a long-term basis and to be committed to working for unity, we have to learn how to remain close to suffering, how to hold on in situations of pain. We have to discover compassion. Jesus puts compassion at the heart of the new life he came to bring: "Be compassionate as your Father is compassionate. Do not judge and you will not be judged; do not condemn and you will not be condemned; forgive and you will be forgiven" (Luke 6:36–37). To be compassionate means to walk with those in pain, to understand them, to comfort them, and especially to love them and remain with them just as Mary remained with Jesus at the foot of the cross (see John 19). There was a force of love in her that allowed her to stay while the others were running away.

— "Letter to my brothers and sisters in L'Arche
and in Faith and Light," March 1999, *OLT*, 459

In chapter 53 of Isaiah, the "suffering servant" is described as disfigured, scorned, without beauty. Jesus on the cross is also disfigured; he lives the mystery of complete abandonment: "My Father, My Father, why have you forsaken me?"

Often the handicapped person also lives this mystery of abandonment. He is often disfigured, scorned, and not very beautiful to look at. This rejection and abandonment push him to anguish and confusion. His despair, his aggressiveness, or his anger are compensations for this unbearable anguish. He is an open wound, forced to keep others at a distance.

Mary is standing there, close to her crucified son. She does nothing; she can do nothing for him. She is there, present to him. She looks at him....

She lives his agony but at the same time, through her eyes, she affirms him and encourages him to live this moment fully. For his hour has come, the hour for which he had come into the world. And that hour is for the glory of his Father and for the salvation of the world. Mary does not slip into sadness, completely withdrawn in herself. She is there, sustaining Jesus to the very end. Together they live the mystery of Redemption. She is not scandalized as Peter was by Jesus' weakness and vulnerability. She has already known his weakness but in another way, when she was with him as a little child....

Mary teaches us that when we are close to a child or to an adult who has been completely broken, full of anguish, one for whom it seems we can do nothing, it is important to stay there, to be with him. Through our presence, a warm, loving faithful presence, we can give him or her some strength and peace; we can help them to continue on. We are called to carry him or her in the apparent inutility of their sufferings, without any hatred in our hearts, but with deep serenity and in a spirit of forgiveness. We are to be present to the child who has been innocently wounded, disfigured, beaten, and rejected. We are to trust and to have a heart surrendered to God, in the face of the unfathomable mystery of human suffering.   —*LWP,* 20–22

When I was living in the Forestière, I was given a text by Carl Jung, the analytical psychologist and disciple of Freud. It was a letter he had written to a young Christian woman, which I quote from memory. He said something like this, referring to the words of Jesus in Matthew 25:

I admire Christians,
because when you see someone
who is hungry or thirsty,
you see Jesus.

When you welcome a stranger,
someone who is "strange,"
you welcome Jesus.
When you clothe someone who is naked,
you clothe Jesus.
What I do not understand, however,
is that Christians never seem to recognize Jesus
in their own poverty.
You always want to do good to the poor outside you
and at the same time you deny the poor person
living inside you.
Why can't you see Jesus in your own poverty,
in your own hunger and thirst?
In all that is "strange" inside you:
in the violence and the anguish that are beyond your control!
You are called to welcome all this, not to deny its existence,
but to accept that it is there and to meet Jesus there.

Jung's letter helped me to realize that I cannot welcome and receive Jesus unless I welcome my own weakness, my poverty, and my deepest needs. I cannot accept the wounds of Innocente, Eric, and Lucien unless I am open and accept my own wounded self and seek help. Can I truly be compassionate toward them if I am not compassionate toward myself?   —BTS, 63–64

I do not believe we can truly enter into our own inner pain and wounds and open our hearts to others unless we have had an experience of God, unless we have been touched by God. We must be touched by the Father in order to experience, as the prodigal son did, that no matter how wounded we may be, we are loved. And not only are we loved, but we too are called to heal and to liberate. This healing power in us will not come from our capacities and our riches, but in and through our poverty. We are called to discover that God can bring peace, compassion and love through our wounds.   —FBC, 21

Old Age and Death

The end of life is similar to the beginning with the need to be held and to open up our being. This part of our life has to do with loss as we gradually lose our hair, our teeth, our memory, our job, our health, our energy, our friends, and eventually our life.

The return to the awareness of our weakness can be tragic and we can get very angry: angry at our body, angry at our destiny, angry at everybody. All this anger, grief, and depression surface because we cannot accept our vulnerability. If we cannot accept this, then we cannot have a true experience of communion with another where our hearts are linked and we are being loved for who we are.

The last part of life involves losing our capacity to do things, and as we lose these capacities, there rises up deep inside of us again our vulnerability and our dependency.

I am no longer there as someone powerful. I am no longer there as someone highly capable. I am no longer there to be admired. I am again like a little child in need. I need to trust you. I need you to love me. I need to be in communion with you. I need you because I am old. I need you because I am sick. I need you because I am in the hospital. I need your hand. I need your love.

This is the mystery of life, from the littleness and vulnerability of the child to the littleness and vulnerability of old age with that period in the middle where we think we are important and we think we are strong. The fundamental question behind this process is, "Who are we really throughout all that?"

—*ILWH*, 15–16

Whatever turns life takes, old age remains a time of suffering. Some old people grow more gentle and kind; they live communion and become more human. Some grandparents are surrounded by their children and their grandchildren. But today, in our affluent countries, there are more and more grandparents who cannot stay with their children. They feel lonely and abandoned. So today, many old people are filled with sadness and inner emptiness. Many have been widowed, and live with the constant pain of having lost their lifelong companion. Many spend their time in front of the television, because it helps to kill time, or else they focus all their attention on one person, becoming desperately possessive of them and refusing them their freedom. They live in boredom, depression, and fear. Many have had to retire to old people's homes, cut off from the world, from young people, from their friends, and from the environment they are familiar with, without any cultural, emotional, or spiritual input. Many old people suffer intensely. They feel useless, unwanted, a burden to their children. They lack the strength, energy, and interest to read. They wait for others to do things for them. It takes very little to make them panic. All the feelings of broken communion that we have already described in the child resurface in their consciousness: feelings of guilt, worthlessness, depression, and rebellion.

Lately, I had the privilege of being close to two old people, my mother and Father Thomas. Both of them were in many ways full of peace and serenity, welcoming reality and other people, and above all those who were distressed or lonely. But how both of them suffered, and how they were sometimes filled with anguish during the last months and years of their lives! The lack of energy, the consciousness of their limitations, the lack of sensitivity in people close to them, a world which seemed to pass them by or leave them feeling lonely, lost, and helpless, sometimes sent them into paroxysms of anguish and inner suffering, in which nobody could really reach them. What can we say about this final anguish, this terrible feeling of being abandoned and unwanted, of dying an inner death? Perhaps the fuller a life has been with light, clarity, friends, and success, the more terrible the emptiness and anguish of old age seem.

I have begun to feel these pangs of anguish: when the nights are long and I cannot sleep; when I do not have the energy to think, pray, or read; when I feel jumpy and on edge; when my

imagination becomes wild, mad, and out of control; when feelings of fear, panic, and guilt rise up. The night sometimes seems
so long, and the dawn so far away!

Of course, I can still try to offer up to God all the pain, but
that offering seems so little and inadequate. Faith is so delicate
a thread, but it permits me to live in hope.   — *OJH*, 133–34

Do we really see the gift of old people or are they just senior citizens that we put in a corner? Have they not become
more wise, more contemplative, more prayerful? Today we talk
about senior citizens or the golden age. You would not say
that about wine. You would not say senior wine. No, it is old
wine. There is good taste to it. It is mature. There is a maturity
to old people. They have something to say. You find this very
beautifully in the African culture, where they honor old people
because they are considered to be closer to God.   — *ILWH*, 49

Our bodies are so fragile and vulnerable. If a little bit of metal
comes into my heart, then I die. It is the makeup of my body.
One of the things that we sometimes forget, possibly more in
North America than anywhere else, is that death is inscribed
in our lives. At the age of twenty-three or twenty-four, we are
losing a hundred thousand cells in our brain every day that are
not being replaced. As I get older my brain gets smaller and that
is the same for the liver, the heart, and the kidneys. Death is not
an accident that should not happen. Death is not one of those
things that is all wrong.

We have to discover that loss is part of our nature. Loss is
part of our being. Death is part of what is most intrinsic in us.
We have to learn that life and death are joined together; in some
mysterious way they are intimately linked. As we are called to
welcome life, so we are also called to welcome death. We have
to love this human nature which is ours. We must come to love
our masculinity and our femininity. We cannot change our bodies. Maybe I can put on a plastic nose because my nose is not

too nice but that does not alter what is essential. I am the height and the breadth of what is given to me. Inside this body there is the movement to life, but there is also the movement to decay. There is the movement toward death. But let us not be frightened. Let us try to understand what it is about. Let us find the force, the inner force in our hearts to welcome all that is broken and marked with pain and death. We need to discover that we can walk with people in pain. — *ILWH*, 39–40

The death of someone we love is always painful. To love is to carry another within us, to keep a special place in our heart for him or her. This spiritual space is nourished by a physical presence; death, then, tears out a part of our own heart and puts us in a place of loneliness. Those who deny the suffering of death have never truly loved; they live in a spiritual illusion. To celebrate death, then, is not to deny the pain and the grief it involves; it is to give space to live it, to speak about it, and even to sing of it. It is to give mutual support, looking the reality in the face and placing all in the heart of God in deep trust. Jesus did not come to abolish suffering and death, but to show us the way to live them.

In L'Arche communities, we are often called to face the reality of death. We see both wrenching, cruel, accidental deaths, and sometimes gentler, predictable deaths, anticipated by sickness and failing strength.

There is a way of announcing a death to the community which brings peace. In our community we have a vigil of prayer where we speak together of the one who has just died and often show slides. Wherever possible we keep watch with the body and give an important place to the funeral Mass. In November, the month when, traditionally, we commemorate those who have died, we share our memories of them, taking time to visit the graves of parents and to pray there. Hiding the reality of death is unhealthy and can create deep-seated fears. As we become freer to speak of our fears, we begin the process of liberation from them. — *MW*, 132

Mission of People with Disabilities

The vision of L'Arche is precisely this: to help people with handicaps to own their worth and beauty, to help them to have confidence in themselves, with their particular gifts, to grow and do beautiful things, to change the negative images they have of themselves into positive ones.   — OJH, 108

I am deeply moved as I witness the growth toward wholeness and the holiness of the people with disabilities with whom I live. Some of us have been living together now for twenty years and more. They are men and women of real maturity. When young people come to help in L'Arche, we find they are much less mature. We see a discrepancy in the maturity between those who have a handicap and those who have come to help. So many young people coming to L'Arche today do not know how to make choices or have too many choices; often they are not sure of the meaning of their lives; they themselves are deeply broken.
                                   — FBC, 22–23

We are used to being told that weak people need strong people. This is obvious. But inner unity and healing come about when strong people become aware of their need of the weak. The weak awaken and reveal the heart; they awaken energies of tenderness and compassion, kindness and communion. They awaken the source of life....
  This transformation involves a succession of inner deaths, suffering, possibly moments of rebellion. It is not easy. It requires time and constant effort to remain faithful to communion. But this leads to the discovery of our true humanity, and so to a deep inner liberation. In discovering the beauty and light hidden in those who are weak, the strong begin to discover the beauty and light in their own weakness. And more than this; they discover that weakness is a place that favors love and communion, it is the place where God dwells. They discover God hidden in littleness, and this is an even greater liberation.   — OJH, 220–22

3

" . . . One Heart at a Time"
Transformation of the Individual Person

How do human beings find transformation? Unique to Vanier's articulation of the human person is "the secret." The importance of our "secret" is perhaps unexpected from someone so committed to community and shared life. To Vanier, however, every heart has a secret that is known only to God. Community life does not expose or demand revelation of our closest, sacred self, but rather should honor and protect the mystery of each person. This leads to selections of Vanier's writings about the human heart, its life and its wounds, including Vanier's memorable eulogy at Henri Nouwen's funeral in Holland. The following section addresses specific struggles: loneliness, fear, depression, sexuality, and waiting. These complex experiences are not just discouraging or hopeless: rather they are the raw material of our common humanity and resources in our yearnings for transformation. The chapter concludes with Vanier's practical reflections about freedom and liberation.

OUR SECRET

Each person has his secret and mystery, his particular journey, his vocation to grow. Certainly, many people never achieve full maturity, but each can make a little progress toward establishing his identity and becoming open to others. The important thing is not that we should achieve human perfection — far from it — but that we should set out on the road toward it through acts of openness and love, kindness and communion. Every person today, in whatever situation he finds himself, in his home or at work, can perform such acts.

As we have already said, there are things that are predetermined in human beings and things that are not. Identity and human growth are arrived at through choices: choices of friends and of the values we want to live by, the choice of where we put down roots, the choice to accept responsibility.

The first choice, at the root of all human growth, is the choice to accept ourselves; to accept ourselves as we are, with our gifts and abilities, but also our shortcomings, inner wounds, darkness, faults, mortality; to accept our past and family and environment, but equally our capacity for growth; to accept the universe with its laws, and our place at the heart of this universe. Growth begins when we give up dreaming about ourselves and accept our humanity as it is, limited and poor but also beautiful. Sometimes, the refusal to accept ourselves hides real gifts and abilities. The dangerous thing for human beings is to want to be other than they are, to want to be someone else, or even to want to be God. We need to be ourselves, with our gifts and abilities, our capacity for communion and co-operation. This is the way to be happy.   — *OJH*, 148–19

When I discover that I am accepted and loved as a person, with my strengths and weaknesses, when I discover that I carry within myself a secret, the secret of my uniqueness, then I can begin to open up to others and respect their secret. The fear of others begins to dissolve; inclusion, friendship, and a feeling of brotherhood/sisterhood begins to emerge. As we become more conscious of the uniqueness of others, we become aware of our common humanity. We are all fundamentally the same, no matter what our age, gender, race, culture, religion, limits, or disabilities may be. We all have vulnerable hearts and need to be loved and appreciated. We have all been wounded in our hearts and have lost trust in what is deepest in us. We all want to be valued and to be able to develop our capacities and grow to greater freedom.   — BH, 82

Those who accompany others also need to recognize the boundaries of their role. It is not necessary to know everything. There must be respect for the private space and the inner secret of each person's being.   — MW, 46

A time of community sharing doesn't mean a total openness. We all have a secret which only God, our closest friends, or our spiritual guide knows. Married couples have a secret they do not share with their children or other members of the family. So our meetings are there for us to share what we are living in community. The line that separates our personal secret from what should be shared is, however, a very fine one. That is why some people find it impossible to share at all.   — CG, 286–87

As Jesus says to each one of us, "Come and follow me," as he calls us by our name with that incredible voice of tenderness calling us to freedom, he will reveal four secrets to us, and each one of those secrets will at the same time reveal and calm our fears.

The first secret pertains to his own self, his own person. His body is the temple of the Spirit of God. He is that place where God resides. He is the resting place of God. He is God on earth. He is the Word made flesh.

The second secret that Jesus reveals to us is that our bodies are also the temple of God, and this is an incredible secret. Many people do not know this secret. Some people can perhaps admire and find it wonderful that the body of Christ is the temple of the divinity, but they are frightened of their own bodies. They are filled with guilt, perhaps because of a consciousness of the tomb inside of them. They cannot believe that their body is the temple where God resides. "My soiled body, a place where God can live?" So many people out of fear refuse that truth. They cannot bear that truth.

The third secret of Jesus is that he is hidden in a very special way in the poor, the broken, and the suffering. "Whatever you do to the least of my brethren, the smallest, the most broken of my brethren, you have done it to me. When I was in prison you visited me. When I was sick you helped me. When I was hungry and thirsty, you gave me to eat and drink. When I was a stranger, you welcomed me. When I was naked you clothed me."

The mystery is that Jesus is hidden in the poorest and in the weakest but also in the poverty of our own being. At one moment Jesus took a little child and said, "Whoever welcomes one of these little ones in my name, welcomes me. And whoever welcomes me welcomes the Father." God is hidden in the face of that little child. That little child is Jesus.

There is fear in our hearts at this thought, for if Jesus is hidden in the hearts of the smallest, the weakest, and the suffering, if he is hidden in my poverty, then that is truly a revolution. The poor then are at the heart of the church. The poor are at the heart of humanity. They are not meant to be pushed aside. This revolution means a complete reordering of the political, social, and religious structures. It means breaking down the fortress of prejudice and the walls of security. Jesus is breaking all this down to bring us into the insecurity of love and the insecurity of communion, where God is present and calling us.

The fourth secret of Jesus concerns the meaning of pain. We have been taught to use tranquilizers to calm pain. We have been taught that pain and suffering, loss and grief are the worst thing that can happen to us. The whole vision of Jesus is to reveal to us not to run away but to walk toward the person in pain. If you run away you will enter a world of dreams. You will cut yourself off from reality. If you walk toward the person in pain, there is a completely new vision of the world. It is the discovery that pain can be enfolded in love, that pain and suffering can become a gift that I can give to God and to humanity. — *ILWH,* 88–90

We all need unique and personal relationships. I am deeply moved by the sensitivity of heart in some of the men and women with disabilities that I have known, like David, who deeply loves Rachael, a young assistant who left to live in a developing country. Time and again, he sends her part of his salary "for the children with learning disabilities in her center." He says: "Rachael is my friend; it is because of her that I work." I sense the power and delicacy of the love in his heart as something sacred and divine. This is not a dream, for this love has truly helped him to find a profound balance. It is his secret, and it must be respected.

There is a similar secret in the heart of Richard. He is not a very religious man. He believes, but rarely goes to Mass or to evening prayer. One day, whispering in my ear, he asked me to go with him to the chapel to pray. There he said a prayer of consecration to the Blessed Virgin Mary, putting himself totally in her hands. I was deeply touched by this gesture.

Laurence, too, never goes to Mass except for funerals, weddings, and important feast days. This is not because he has anything against the Mass; he is simply not in the habit of going. However, he was very touched by the story of Our Lady of La Salette, the apparition of Mary to two children who saw her weeping. "She was like a mother beaten by her children and driven from her home," one of the children said after the apparition. When I welcomed Laurence to L'Arche, he, too, had wept many tears. There was a kind of complicity between him and that woman who had wept on the mountain. It is the secret of his heart.

Many men and women I know in L'Arche have a secret in the depths of their hearts, a secret through which they are linked with someone of the other sex. Whether this person plays the role of father or mother, of big brother or big sister or a beloved for them is not important. What is important is that they love.

I am shocked when I see some people ridiculing the bonds of love which unite a man and a woman with disabilities. Often these are bonds of a secret and sacred tenderness which must be respected. Perhaps they are called to live these bonds only on the level of the heart, in the simplicity of love. It should not be assumed that this relationship must necessarily become physical and sexual as such.   — *MW,* 118–19

THE HEART —
ITS LIFE AND ITS WOUNDS

The heart, the metaphorical heart, the basis of all relationships, is what is deepest in each one of us. It is my heart that bonds itself to another heart; it leads us out of the restricted belonging, which creates exclusion, to meet and love others just as they are.
                                                            — *BH,* 85

Jesus washes the feet of his disciples not before the meal, which could have been a Jewish custom of purification, but during the meal. Imagine the disciples' surprise when they saw Jesus get up and take off his outer garments in the middle of the Passover meal, which was a particularly solemn occasion. They must have looked at each other in amazement: "What is he doing now?" It was such a strange action!...

As Jesus removes his garments, he is stripping himself as well of any function or social status. Of course, he is Jewish and a teacher and a prophet, so he does have authority and power. But here he presents himself to his disciples just as a person, a friend. Before being Lord and teacher, he is a heart seeking to meet other hearts, a friend yearning to be in communion with friends, a loving person seeking to live in the heart of his friends.

In this domain of the heart, all people are alike. There is no visible hierarchy one could signify by dress. People with or without visible handicaps, the poor and the rich, the young and the old, people with AIDS or in good health, they all are alike and they all have the same dignity. Each one's life and history are sacred. Each person is unique and important. The only hierarchy that remains is one of love, and that remains hidden. (Is that really a hierarchy?) Each person's heart is a mystery. A man in prison may in fact be more loving than his guard or judge, a woman with a handicap more loving than her teacher, or an immigrant more loving than somebody in high office. So at the end of our lives we will be judged by how we have loved, and not by our clothes, or the masks society has imposed on us. We will be judged according to who we really are and not on our job or role in society. As Jesus removes his outer garments, he is reminding us of what is most important in life: our hearts.

— *SS*, 16, 18–19

It is important that we experience
the reality of our limited love;
the reality of our broken hearts.
Only then can we begin to understand
what Jesus was asking his disciples when he said:
"Love one another."
We may react quite quickly....
"No, I can't love that person!"
And Jesus replies:
"But I tell you who are listening:
Love your enemies, do good to those who hate you,
bless those who curse you,
pray for those who treat you badly" (Luke 6:27–28).

It is easy, he tells us, to love those who love us,
who shower us with compliments.
But Jesus is asking us to love our "enemies."
Our enemy is not necessarily some foreigner
but could be someone quite close,
in our own family or community; someone at work.
The "enemy" is someone who seems to threaten us

and prevents us from being ourselves,
someone who blocks our freedom and creativity
and who provokes depression or aggression in us
by their very presence.

When we have some quiet time,
it is important to ask God to show us who is our enemy.
It is perfectly natural for us to have people who have hurt us
and awaken our defense mechanisms —
that is a part of who we are,
part of our common humanity.   —*BTS*, 70–71

To speak of the heart is not to speak of vaguely defined emotions but to speak of the very core of our being. At the core, we all know we can be strengthened and rendered more truthful and more alive. Our hearts can become hard like stone or tender like flesh. We have to create situations where our hearts can be fortified and nourished. In this way, we can be more sensitive to others, to their needs, their cries, their inner pain, their tenderness, and their gifts of love.

Our hearts, however, are never totally pure. People can cry out to be loved, especially if as children they were not loved. There are "loving" relationships that are unhealthy because they are a flight from truth and from responsibility. There are friendships that are unhealthy because one is too frightened to challenge one's friend. These are the signs of the immature heart. An immature heart can lead us to destructive relationships and then to depression and death.

It is only once a heart has become mature in love that it can take the road of insecurity, putting its trust in God. It is a heart that can make wise decisions; it has learned to discern and to take risks that bring life. It can meet other people inside and outside of the place of belonging. It can meet people who have been excluded. It is the heart that helps us to discover the common humanity that links us all, that is even stronger than all that bonds us together as part of a specific group. The heart,

then, foregoes the need to control others. The free heart frees
others.   — *BH*, 87–88

Eulogy for Henri Nouwen

Over the years that I have known Henri, he always brought sur-
prises. You never quite knew what was going to happen! And
he surprised us all Saturday morning. His family had seen how
well he was, and I had talked to him on the phone on Friday
night. Then on Saturday he died.

There was a mystery in Henri. Just forty years ago he was
lying on these steps to be ordained a priest, on these very steps
where his body is lying today. So Henri came home to Holland,
and tomorrow his body will go home to his community. We
all know how important home was for Henri. Henri had many
occasions to speak and to accompany people who were dying. I
feel very moved that I should be asked to say a few words about
Henri in front of his family, his father, brothers, and sister, and
in front of the family of Daybreak and L'Arche, and the family
of his friends.

Having known Henri over a number of years, the first thing I
want to say is that he was a man of great energy, vision, and insight, but also a man of great pain. Anguish often fueled many
of his activities, his movement. In many ways he was a man of
movement. I was always moved when I sensed the depth of his
pain. But Henri had discovered something, for even though in
some ways he was running away from pain, at the same time
he chose to walk through pain; he accepted anguish; he did
not build up barriers to protect himself. In a mysterious way
he was a wounded healer, the name of one of his first books.
Yes, he was a wounded healer and in many ways a wounded
man, searching, yearning, crying out. A brilliant and wounded
man who walked through the years of change in the church
and change in the world because our world is a terribly and
beautifully changing world.

people with disabilities and the brokenness of Henri, between
the wounded heart of people with disabilities and the wounded
heart of Henri and the wounded heart of Christ. So he found
a home and there he became more whole. L'Arche was a gift
for Henri, but Henri was an incredible gift for L'Arche, a gift
of Jesus to L'Arche, the gift of a priest, a compassionate friend.
Henri was a man of compassion. He would go to the end of
the world to help someone in need. He was not a man who
was terribly interested in structures but in people, wounded
people, people in pain, people suffering, old people, people
dying, people with AIDS, ordinary people in their struggles. He
brought light, hope, and comfort to the members of his community and beyond. He shared his life, his gifts, his friends, and
his evolving spirituality with L'Arche people everywhere.

Henri was attracted in a mysterious way to other people, his
pain meeting their pain and both contained the pain of our crucified Christ. He put a word or words on L'Arche, on what we are
living, words that were accessible to people, giving direction to
their lives. He announced something very important: that unity
in our world and in our churches will spring from the poor. . . . He
was a sign of hope, a sign of meaning in a divided world with
divided Christians. . . . There was something prophetic in Henri.
He accepted pain, he chose to walk through pain because it is
the road for all of us. To choose the cross, to walk through the
cross, because never will we discover resurrection unless we walk
through the cross, unless we are stripped.

> — From Jean Vanier's eulogy at Henri Nouwen's funeral
> in Utrecht, September 25, 1996 (unpublished)

THE HUMAN CONDITION

Loneliness

When people are physically well, performing creatively, successful in their lives, loneliness seems absent. But I believe that
loneliness is something essential to human nature; it can only

be covered over; it can never actually go away. Loneliness is part of being human, because there is nothing in existence that can completely fulfill the needs of the human heart.

Loneliness in one form is, in fact, essential to our humanity. Loneliness can become a source of creative energy, the energy that drives us down new paths to create new things or to seek more truth and justice in the world. Artists, poets, mystics, prophets, those who do not seem to fit into the world or the ways of society, are frequently lonely. They feel themselves to be different, dissatisfied with the status quo and with mediocrity, dissatisfied with our competitive world where so much energy goes into ephemeral things. Frequently, it is the lonely man or woman who revolts against injustice and seeks new ways. It is as if a fire is burning within them, a fire fueled by loneliness.

Loneliness is the fundamental force that urges mystics to a deeper union with God. For such people, loneliness has become intolerable but, instead of slipping into apathy or anger, they use the energy of loneliness to seek God. It pushes them toward the absolute. An experience of God quenches this thirst for the absolute but at the same time, paradoxically, whets it, because this is an experience that can never be total; by necessity, the knowledge of God is always partial. So loneliness opens up mystics to a desire to love each and every human being as God loves them.

Loneliness, then, can be a force for good. More frequently, however, loneliness shows other, less positive faces. It can be a source of apathy and depression, and even of a desire to die. It can push us into escapes and addictions in the need to forget our inner pain and emptiness. This apathy is how loneliness most often shows itself in the elderly and in those with disabilities. It is the loneliness we find in those who fall into depression, who have lost the sense of meaning in their lives, who are asking the question born of despair: What is left?

— *BH*, 7–9

Even the most beautiful community can never heal the wound of loneliness that we carry. It is only when we discover that this loneliness can become a sacrament that we touch wisdom, for this sacrament is purification and presence of God. If we stop fleeing from our own solitude, and if we accept our wound, we will discover that this is the way to meet Jesus Christ. It is when we stop fleeing into work and activity, noise, and illusion, and when we remain conscious of our wound, that we will meet God. He is the Paraclete, the One who responds to our cry, which comes from the darkness of our loneliness.

— *CG*, 329–30

Fear

I believe that what is important today is that we uncover the violence within us and discover that under the violence there is something very beautiful. One of the questions that always comes up is "What do we fear?" One of the questions that I like to ask all the people of our communities is, "What are you most frightened of? Is it fear of not being respected? Is it fear of being put aside? Is it fear of not being loved? Is it fear of death?" What is it that we're frightened of? Because from fear and anguish can rise hate and from hate can rise war.

We must learn how to look into our fears because we cannot let ourselves be controlled by fear. We have to look our fears right in the face, and we can't always do it by ourselves. We need to be helped, because if we can't look death and failure in the face, well, then we can never live because to live means to risk, to do things, to have projects that might fail, that might go wrong. We cannot be totally secure for everything; we must discover inside ourselves this power that we have been given to receive the Holy Spirit, not alone, but with others in community, to decide to go forward and to risk things.

— *EO*, 27

Very popular today in our world is a vision of a sentimental, devotional God, a God who blesses us and says, "Everything is all right, and if you love me, if you want to be with me, then you will be rich and you will have no more pain; I will protect you." This vision of a sentimental and romantic God does not address the reality of our lives. There is another vision of God, which is also in favor with some: the God of fear, the God who is a lawgiver, the God in the sky sending down rigid laws and commandments. Here God appears as a policeman giving us a ticket if we speed too much. God appears rigid, judgmental, seeking to punish and to hurt, not a lover, not a friend but someone looking into all the little things we do and hitting us on the hand because we have been disobedient.

This image of God as the lawgiver, the one who chastises and punishes, comes from something very deep in our psyche. The pain of the abandoned child or the pain of the child who has not been welcomed is quickly transformed into guilt and it is this inner pain transformed into guilt that creates this image of a God who is going to punish. It is guilt that creates in us a whole world of fear.

It is fear that makes us run away from pain. It is fear that makes us run away from those who are poor, who are weak and who are sick. It is fear that provides the impetus that pushes us up the ladder, seeking power, prestige, and privilege. It is fear that brings us to the point of loneliness and it is fear that creates the fortress of prejudice and a scale of values that creates a society with the rich and the powerful at the top and the weak and the poor at the bottom.

It is fear that has pushed humanity and entire societies to create false gods, strange gods, gods that crush humanity rather than bring humanity to freedom. I can really understand people who are atheists. I can really understand people who proclaim that they do not believe in God because what they are saying is that they do not believe in false gods. They do not believe in a romantic God that just blesses human beings by making them rich. They do not believe in a God who is going to punish them. Some atheists, who refuse to believe in these false gods, have a deep sense of the human heart and a deep sense of human reality.

Those who do not believe in God have not met the true God, and the true God I believe deeply has been revealed to us by Jesus, who comes to undermine all the fortresses built on fear. Jesus comes to touch our hearts in the deepest craving of our being.   —*ILWH,* 83–84

This fortress of prejudice is based on fear and it is precisely there that Jesus is going to touch us. The central message of Jesus is, "Do not be afraid." When Jesus says, "Do not be afraid," he is undermining the whole fortress of prejudice based on fear. But fear of what? It is fear of my own littleness, of my own heart, which could easily be hurt when I was a child.

The fear exists because, perhaps, I wasn't confirmed or comforted in my vulnerability. Why do parents not confirm or comfort the child? It is because they themselves are wounded. The child inside of them has been hurt. So each of us according to our past, according to the way we were brought up in our family life, have this world of hardness in us. This hardness is crushing our vulnerability and puts up barriers around our heart, around the child in us.   —*ILWH,* 61

Depression

There are times of presence and times of absence in our life of love with the Spirit. There are times when we sense the Spirit of God in us, when we sense a love for the enemy, a death of aggressiveness, a flowing of the peace which is unity among people. And there are times when we are confused, when everything seems hard. At these times we tend to weep and say that God has forgotten us. We forget that the life of love is like the seasons—that there is spring and there is the harshness of winter. We forget that winter is important too, that nature needs to sleep, that frost is necessary for the rebirth of spring. There is the season of rain and the dry season; each complements the other.

We must go through winters of suffering, through times when prayer is hard and people no longer attract us, but spring is not far away. A death in the family, a failure in work, a sickness which brings a new way of life, an unfaithful friend, all these are wounds to the heart that take us into a period of darkness. This darkness is important. We must learn to be strong and peaceful in darkness, not fighting it, but waiting. We must learn to accept this winter as a gift from God, and we will discover that the snow will melt and the flowers come up.

> We know that in everything God works for good with those who love him, who are called according to his purpose.
>
> (Rom. 8:28)

This is how things of the Spirit are — a linking of time and eternity, with moments of communion and moments of fidelity. There are the spring times that are moments of communion and peace and rejoicing in the Spirit. And there are times of fidelity when we are close to Jesus, he who agonized more than any of us, and we say, "Let this cup pass from me; nevertheless, not as I will, but as thou wilt" (Matt. 25:39).

We have to be very careful in times of winter not to be seduced by compensations. We may spend too much time in useless leisure or unending talk because of our solitude and our anguish. If we are celibate, we may dream that things would be better if we were married. If we live in a large community, we may dream that life would be happier in a small apartment. Some of our dreams may be true. But we have to be careful of winter dreams.

We must learn to live through the winter, for it is a profound part of any relationship. No community of people is really born until it has worked through tension and aggression. It is when we have worked through these — whether we are a community, husband and wife, or collaborators in work — that we find each other in a new way.

So it is with the Spirit of Jesus. His first call is a call of peace and quietness, and we go forth with great rejoicing. But then he wants us to grow strong in our love and our faith. He wants us to grow in a love that is never shaken.

Who shall separate us from the love of Christ? Shall tribulation, or distress, or persecution, or famine, or nakedness, or peril, or sword? As it is written, "For thy sake we are being killed all the day long; we are regarded as sheep to be slaughtered."

> No, in all these things we are more than conquerors through him who loved us. For I am sure that neither death, nor life, nor angels, nor principalities, nor things present, nor things to come, nor powers, nor height, nor depth, nor anything else in all creation, will be able to separate us from the love of God in Christ Jesus our Lord.
>
> (Rom. 8:35–39)

To be able to say this, we have to go through the strengthening times, which are the times of winter. We have to discover gradually the anguish at the heart of the universe, to discover the role of sacrifice, the role of suffering, the role of the offering.

— *BNA*, 140–42

But there is a deeper sadness that shows itself when a person feels frustrated or hurt, or when he or she experiences a setback, an emotional crisis, great tension, conflict, or grief that seems unbearable. The person feels overwhelmed by sadness; an inner death surges forth from the depths of their being. . . . Initially this loss of energy resembles the grieving process described above, but the depth of pain and sadness seems to be out of all proportion to the event that has prompted it, Furthermore, unlike in times of grief, the sadness does not ease with time or with new activity; on the contrary, inner paralysis seems to increase. The person feels imprisoned in a world of darkness, completely cut off from others. Depression is an illness that we cannot treat by ourselves. We need help to recover from it.   — *SBD*, 11–13

Depression is a painful reality, a crisis, but at the same time crisis can bring us to greater freedom if we discover how to live with it and how to move toward healing.

Depression, such as we have described, is the emergence in our consciousness of a hidden pain that has its origin in our early childhood. These hidden sufferings determine many of our attitudes, even if we are not aware of it. They prevent us from being free. They are like a huge weight on our hearts, a poison in our blood. Then one day, we become more aware, terribly aware of this inner pain, and it is like an infection that turns into an abscess. We can then name the "disease" and seek its origins and the way toward healing.

When depression becomes more visible, better accepted as such, it can lead us toward a genuine liberation of the heart. It obliges us to stop and look at what is really important in our own lives and in life in general. It puts us in touch with our deepest need, the need for love and a communion of hearts, but also with our fears of them. It helps us to see that, above and beyond all human relationships, it is possible for us to drink from the source of the universe and of life.   — *SBD, 75–77*

To get out of depression, which is a kind of imprisonment, first of all we must want to do so. We also need a good therapist and, even more important, a network of friends who love and accept us. They will sustain us in difficult moments, when we feel particularly fragile; depression can make us feel so very vulnerable. The slightest setback or sense of rejection, or a traumatic event, can nourish or revive our sense of powerlessness. Friends can help us to walk through the pain.

Friends are sometimes unable, however, to understand the depth of our pain, the "hell" we are living. They might think they do, but we know that they do not! ... Friends are called to walk with those in depression and not to make glib remarks. People who have suffered seem to understand much better the pain of other people.   — *SBD, 87–89*

Sexuality

It is true that in L'Arche we do not want to belittle sexual relationships. We do not believe that they are just a therapeutic
means or a way for someone to express himself and to liberate
a physical need. We believe in the beauty, in the gravity, and, I
would say, the mystery of sexuality as an expression of a profound communion between two persons and the gift of their
being to each other, in a reciprocal and permanent commitment.
We believe that when this is not the case, and when the sexual
act is completely separated from the relationship of communion
between two people, it is no longer a source of unity for them.
When the sexual act is separated from the heart and from relationship, the other person becomes an object. There is no longer
anything personal in the act. There is no giving; only taking.
The sexual act in this context loses the beauty of its potential to
deepen the unity and affection of the couple.

   To affirm such a belief is an enormous challenge in these
times when sexuality is so vulgarized by the mass media and
when others propose that those with disabilities should be given
every help and material means to exercise their right to sexuality and to pleasure. My fear today is that, instead of helping
those with disabilities to discover the love of a couple, with
all its intimacy and the bond it implies, they are led toward
the mirage of easy sexuality without responsibility, without a
permanent bond between two people, without true fecundity.
This form of sexuality finally leads them to disappointment and
a new isolation, because it does not respond to their deepest
needs, to their thirst for a covenant relationship. The attrac-
tion of man for woman, and of woman for man, is profound.
There is a thirst for tenderness that nourishes itself through sexuality and that leads to it. But for that sexuality to be truly
human, springing up from relationship and strengthening it,
people must have a clear awareness of their identity, knowing
who they are and what they wish to make of their lives.

                                                  —*MW*, 131–32

Then I saw a new heaven and a new earth; for the first heaven and the first earth had passed away, and the sea was no more. And I saw the holy city, new Jerusalem, coming down out of heaven from God, prepared as a bride adorned for her husband; and I heard a loud voice from the throne saying, "Behold, the dwelling of God is with men. He will dwell with them, and they shall be his people, and God himself will be with them; he will wipe away every tear from their eyes, and death shall be no more, neither shall there be mourning nor crying nor pain any more, for the former things have passed away."

(Rev. 21:1–4)

But on earth we must continue as pilgrims of hope, sometimes walking in the night. That is why our constant cry must be, "Come." And that is why also the whole of scripture ends with:

The Spirit and the Bride say, "Come." And let him who hears say, "Come." And let him who is thirsty come, let him who desires take the water of life without price.

(Rev. 22:17)

Jesus calls us all to live this experience of love in some way. But some are called to live it more deeply. For this is in reality the experience of the alliance and the covenant. Our God is a lover. So it is normal that Jesus will call forth some to virginity and to celibacy, so that they might offer themselves totally in all their being to the touch and the hope of the alliance. Those who answer his call to celibacy are, in some way, a special sign of the uniqueness of this love of God, though of course, those who are married can and do have this experience of love.

Celibacy is particularly difficult in a world like ours, which does not believe the message of Jesus and which knows less about the communion and fidelity of love than it does about sexuality, a world which can mock at love through television and cinema. This is why it is important that Christian communities come forth where people can live celibacy, not as a

called to change the world but to love people, to be close to them and to live in communion with them.   —*ILWH,* 107–11

As we learn to wait, we begin to discover the whole mystery of creation. On the one side God is so great, so beautiful and we are so small and so poor. We discover that God is at the beginning and at the end of all things. He is the alpha and the omega. He is the seed and he is the cedar tree. He is the beauty of all our world, and as I disappear into the earth, the sun will continue to rise and to set. I am part of something much bigger, much wider, much more beautiful than I can ever imagine. Our God is making this world move in love. God, independent of our world but totally united in some mysterious way to our hearts and to the hearts of this world, is present and is the eternal "now."...

As I discover the vastness of the project of history and the littleness of my being, I discover that it is all right simply to wait. It is all right just to be as I am, for there is something much larger than my vision and my program, no matter how large it may appear in this world. God is there at the source and the end of all things. And as I wait, somewhere I am saying, "I trust you."

Each one of us is waiting. Creation is waiting. Humanity in its totality is waiting for the promise. But sometimes we forget that Jesus is also waiting, that God is waiting for the beloved to return. Jesus is waiting and sometimes, we may imagine, in tears, as he weeps over this broken humanity saying, "If you had but known the gift of God. If you had but known the message of peace."   —*ILWH,* 112–13

TRANSFORMATION— FREEDOM AND LIBERATION

To be free is to know who we are, with all that is beautiful, all the brokenness in us; it is to love our own values, to embrace

them, and to develop them; it is to be anchored in a vision and a
truth but also to be open to others and, so, to change. Freedom
lies in discovering that the truth is not a set of fixed certitudes
but a mystery we enter into, one step at a time. It is a process
of going deeper and deeper into an unfathomable reality.

— BH, 117–18

When we discover that we are all part of a larger family,
united in a common humanity,
and that over and above us and within us
there is a universal truth and justice,
where the God of Compassion and Goodness is present,
then we find ourselves on the journey to freedom.
When we have an experience of the love of God
and the God of Love,
we begin to discover how precious each person
is in God's plan for humanity.

With all our beauty and brokenness,
each one of us is important.
We can be ourselves and let the beauty in us grow.
We are not the center of the world —
and we do not have to be!
We are part of a broken humanity,
and in the company of others,
we can stand up and continue the quest
for freedom, truth, and peace.

Jesus says to Pilate:
"I was born and came into the world
in order to give witness to the truth."

Pilate replies:
"What is truth?" (John 19:37–38).

That is the question.

Truth is what we see and touch and experience.
It is not something we invent,
but something we humbly receive and welcome,
something that is bigger, greater than ourselves.

But truth is often hidden from us,
which is why it takes time and the help of others
to discern the truth.
We often find truth only after we choose to let go of
some of the illusions of life that we may still have.
It takes time to find inner freedom —
this is the ongoing work of a lifetime.
I do not have this freedom yet,
but my hope is to continue to keep my heart open
to receive it.   —*DMJ*, 160–61

We know what success is, but are we seeking success at the
risk of damaging our humanity? I find that one of the most important things we are called to do as peacemakers is to find a
style of living. How do we live? I see so many people in France
who have to travel an hour and a half by car to work. They
work and then they come home and they are absolutely pooped!
When they come back home at perhaps eight o'clock at night
they just put themselves in front of the television, because there
is too much stress and too much fatigue. What does it mean to
be stuck in front of the television and to receive images without
any dialogue? We should try to find a style of life where we live
peacefully, where we can find silence, because we cannot be at
peace unless we cherish silence; silence in the family where we
can be together and love each other.

In the prayer of Ecclesiastes there is time to be silent and time
to talk, but talk must always come from the place of silence and
not from a place of aggressiveness and power.

It is quite obvious that when we are stressed, when we are
fatigued, when we don't know how to eat well, when we don't

know how to eat together and have fun, then we lose something of what it means to be a human being. If we want to
be people of peace we have to know what it means to be a
human being, to be mature, to love people, to contemplate, to
love nature, to love children, and to have fun with children.
If parents are too busy working and never have time to go on
their hands and knees and play with their children, then they
are losing something of their humanity.   —EO, 42–43

I would suggest that there are three basic principles underlying
forgiveness in the move toward reconciliation.

Principle 1: There can be no forgiveness of ourselves or of
others unless we believe that we are all part of a common
humanity. What this means in practical terms is that no one individual, no one group is superior to others.... In order to enter
the path of forgiveness, we have to lose our feelings of both superiority and inferiority. Each of us has hurt another, each of
us has been hurt. And so we must own and take responsibility
for our lives as well as for the future. We are all called upon to
stand up and take our place freely in the world.

Principle 2: To forgive means to believe that each of us can
evolve and change, that human redemption is possible....

Principle 3: To forgive means to yearn for unity and peace.
Unity is the ultimate treasure. It is the place where, in the garden of humanity, each one of us can grow, bear fruit, and give
life....

At the heart of the process of forgiveness is the desire to
be liberated from negative passions, from sharp dislikes and
hatred. This is a desire that starts us on the road to true forgiveness. Having proposed three principles of forgiveness, let
me now propose five steps.

The first step is the refusal to seek revenge. No more "an eye
for an eye and a tooth for a tooth."

The second step is the genuine, heartfelt hope that the oppressor be liberated. The victim cannot change the heart that is

filled with fear and hate, but one may hope and pray that one day the oppressor's heart of stone may become a heart of flesh.

The third step is the desire to understand the oppressors: how and why their indifference or hardness of heart has developed, and how they might be liberated.

The fourth step is the recognition of our own darkness. We, too, have hurt people and perhaps have contributed to the hardness of the oppressors.

The fifth step is patience. It takes time for a victim to be freed from blockage and hatred; it takes time for an oppressor to evolve and to change.

Reconciliation is a bilateral affair; it is the completion of the forgiveness process, the coming together of the oppressed and the oppressor, each one accepting the other, each acknowledging their fears and hatreds, each accepting that the path of mutual love is the only way out of a world of conflict.

— BH, 152–55

Forgiveness is to say yes to someone. To refuse to forgive is to say no; it is separation. Forgiveness is to recognize the bond, to accept the other person just as he or she is. It is to let life begin to flow. But that is not always easy because I myself am broken. When someone has hurt me and has caused me inner pain and anguish there is a tendency to cover up my vulnerability with the power of the "no."

But we cannot really forgive without a power that comes from inside us....

I think the whole message of Jesus, why the Word became flesh, why he dwelt among us, why he lived simply among us for thirty years, is to teach us one lesson — to forgive. That is the message of Jesus — forgiveness.

How can I forgive somebody who has hurt me? How can I forgive somebody who has hurt one of my loved ones? The very heart of the message of Jesus is, "Love your enemy; pray for those who persecute you; be kind to those who revile you and

who hurt you." That is incredible. But before it is a command-
ment, it is a promise. He is saying, "I will help you and I will
teach you. I will give you a new strength and I will give you a
new love." The whole of the yearning of Christ is to transform
violence into tenderness, so that separateness can become unity.
Jesus wants each one of us to forgive the enemy but first of all
he forgives us, enabling us to forgive ourselves and giving us the
power to forgive the enemy.   — ILWH, 105–6

To advance, we need to be determined, to make definite efforts
and to struggle not to be overcome by fear, depression, and apathy. These efforts, which constitute forgiveness, begin with our
refusal to wish that the enemy might be wiped out, die, or disappear, and the recognition that he has a right to exist and live
because he is a human being with a heart and feelings....
    Some time ago now, I was in a monastery. In the monastery
refectory talking was not allowed. In front of me there was a
very well dressed woman of about fifty-five. She ate like a pig!
As I watched her, feelings of irritation and anger welled up in
me. Why did she, and the way she ate, have this effect on me?
I realized that I had a problem. And, seeing that it was disturbing my peace, I tried to understand it. This woman was clearly
anguished and suffering. The way she ate was surely the result
of anguish. And so, within myself, I was able to turn judgment
and rejection into compassion.
    The process of transforming the enemy into someone whom
we respect and accept takes time, effort, and discipline. Peace
does not drop out of the sky. Certainly, it comes from a hidden
force of God, but it comes also through the thousand efforts
which we make daily, efforts to accept others just as they are,
to forgive them, to accept ourselves also, with all our wounds
and fragility, to discover that the enemy is within us, to discover
also how to cope with our wounds, fears, and anguish, and use
them in a positive way.   — OJH, 234–35

4

The Christian Life

*These selections offer a window into Vanier's Christian spiri-
tuality. Although at first glance it would seem that Jean Vanier
focuses more on human beings in community than the silence
of prayer, he writes deeply about the faith and practices that
sustain him: prayer and retreat, following Jesus, reading the
Gospels.*

PRAYER AND RETREAT

I have come to see that to pray is above all to dwell in Jesus
and to let Jesus dwell in me.
It is not first and foremost to say prayers,
but to live in the now of the present moment,
in communion with Jesus.
Prayer is a place of rest and quiet.
When we love someone,
don't we love just to be with each other,
to be present one to another?
Now and again we may say a word of affection,
we will be attentive to each other and listen to each other,
but it is essentially a place of silence.   —*DMJ*, 358

Let's stop running. Let's stop running away from ourselves and from the deepest part of our beings. Let's stop running away from this earth and this beautiful world that is ours. Let's stop running away from each other. Perhaps...we should go and sit under the tree. And there, let us just listen to the birds and to the music that underlies the song of the birds, because there we will hear the music of God.

Let us simply stop and start listening to our own hearts. There we will touch a lot of pain. We will possibly touch a lot of anger. We will possibly touch a lot of loneliness and anguish. Then we will hear something deeper. We will hear the voice of Jesus; we will hear the voice of God. We will discover that the heart of Christ, in some mysterious way, is hidden in my heart and there, we will hear, "I love you. You are precious to my eyes and I love you." — *ILWH*, 82

Prayer is not the unthinking mumbling of meaningless words, but the opening of our hearts to the Eternal Love that is the source of all creation. Prayer is the response of the heart to God who is Love. Prayer is the opening of one's heart to peace, to the peace of God, the opening of one's mind and one's heart to the Spirit of God. Prayer is the desire that we might be filled with this spirit of love and of justice and of peace. It is the offering of ourselves to God, who is Love, that we might become the poor instruments of his love, that we might radiate throughout our land and to everyone we know the peace, the compassion, the sweetness, the tenderness and the mercy of God. We all have, we know, a huge thirst for the spirit of God. We all have a thirst for the love of God. Against the problems we face, our weakness is so great. That's why we should go humbly before God and say, "Give me your spirit. I am very weak. Help me in my decisions. The seriousness and the gravity of the hour demand it. I desire only one thing, that is, that you will give peace and gentleness. Give the truth of your love. Help me. Give strength to my poverty, give strength that I may be courageous in front of others. Give me your spirit."

God loves us just as we are
and wants to reveal how deeply he respects us.
During one of our community weekends in northern France,
an assistant asked Frank, a man with disabilities,
if he prayed.
He answered "Yes."
"What do you do when you pray, Frank?"
"I listen."
"What does God say to you?"
"God says to me, 'You are my beloved son,' " he replied.
That is what we discover in prayer:
we are a beloved son, a beloved daughter, of God.
God wants to be united to us,
to reveal his presence to us...

God's presence is also just as real
within *our* weakness and *our* poverty too.   — *BTS*, 45–46

My three weeks' stay in the monastery is coming to an end. I
was tired when I arrived, as the month of July had been quite
heavy. I immediately entered into silence, which is a milieu or
atmosphere that gives me new life. I felt like a fish in water and
I really drank of the water of silence. I rediscovered time, not as
a space too small for everything that has to be fitted in, but time
as a touch of eternity, a presence which, like silence, is a milieu,
a place for communion and intimacy that always goes beyond
time. Now I feel rested and blessed, blessed by Jesus and by the
gift of L'Arche and of Faith and Light, blessed by the gift of life
and of the universe. I feel ready to go back into daily life, back
into the world of struggle and pain, the world of injustice and
evil. That does not mean that here in the monastery I have not
been in touch with all that is dark and painful within my own
heart. I ask forgiveness of each one I might have hurt during this
past year. Here in the monastery, I feel as though I am wrapped
in the cloak of God's forgiveness, which is a cloak that keeps

me peaceful and joyful on the path toward greater union with the Father.

I have been meditating on the life of Jesus, who came to love each person, who is concerned with each person, especially with those who feel lost, excluded, impoverished, abandoned, locked in anguish. He did not come first of all to confirm laws or support institutions (though laws and institutions are important). Jesus came to live in communion with each and every human heart.   —Letter of September 1992, *OLT,* 390–91

We have to be careful during a retreat. We can listen to the music of the word of Jesus and tell ourselves how nice these thoughts are. We can enjoy the company and the food and the talks; we can have a nice spiritual holiday. But we must beware of this holiday, for today in the slums, in the prisons, in hospitals throughout the world, people are sweating it out. If our dream does not become a determination, an action, a yearning, then we can deeply damage ourselves and our brothers and sisters.

The word of Jesus demands action, which means not just doing things, but a certain response to a call. It means a "yes," and we have to be vigilant to see what that "yes" means. God will not be mocked. To play with his things is literally to play with fire, for he is a living loving person and he does not want spectators basking in the sun. The reality of the Gospels is a true reality, and God's call is a real call. His desire a real desire. It is important that each of us respond as the Spirit wants us to respond.   —*BNA,* 107–8

Many of us are not aware of the sacred space within us,
the place where we can reflect and contemplate,
the space from which wonderment can flow
as we look at the mountains, the sky,
the flowers, the fruits and all that is beautiful in our universe,
the space where we can contemplate works of art.

This place, which is the deepest in us all,
is the place of our very personhood,
the place of inner peace where God dwells
and where we receive the light of life and the murmurings
of the Spirit of God.
It is the place in which we make life choices
and from which flows our love for others.

—*DMJ*, 69–70

FOLLOWING JESUS

The message of Jesus is truly good news. It is not, first of all, a
series of laws that we must obey. It is an experience of a loving
encounter with Jesus, in faith and tenderness. This encounter,
which opens us to the universe and to the Father, reveals that
we are precious in the eyes of God. The negative image we
have of ourselves will gradually begin to lose its power over us.
When we discover we are loved by the Father, we can begin
to trust ourselves more; our hearts are on the road to being
healed even though we remain burdened with many untrans-
formed weaknesses and limits. This experience gives hope. The
call of God is within us like a seed; with other people we can
grow in the church, in the community of those who believe in
Jesus and who wish to serve him in the way of the Beatitudes.

—*MW*, 20

Jesus Feeds the Multitude

People are flocking to Jesus; many are being healed.
A huge crowd kept following Jesus because they had seen
the miracles that he was doing for the sick.
Jesus went up the mountain and sat down with his disciples.
Now the Passover, the festival of the Jews, was near.
When he looked up and saw a large crowd
coming toward him,

Jesus said to Philip:
"Where can we buy bread
so that all these people can eat?" (John 6:2–5)
Jesus is concerned about the welfare of all these people.
They have followed him, eating and drinking his words.
Now they must be hungry and exhausted....

Let us go deeper into the significance of this miracle.
Jesus reveals a caring God,
a God who is concerned for our well-being
and wants us to be well,
a God who wants us to be concerned about our own welfare.
Do we eat well? Rest well? Nourish ourselves well?
It is not just a miracle of multiplying food
but also of creating and building a caring community
where people are concerned for one another.

— *DMJ, 118–19*

To those who have experienced God, truly and deeply, he reveals himself as the lover, whether they are Christian or Hindu or Muslim. This is true of St. John of the Cross, Teresa of Avila, and the great mystics of all time. God is the one my heart loves and who communicates to me in some mysterious way a deep interior warmth, a fire, a flowing of living water. He communicates to me a thirst, a desire, an overwhelming peace, for God communicates and gives himself to man in the very depths of his being. When he touches me, he opens me, and at the same time he gives me a thirst to die, for this experience of God is only a taste of the eternal wedding feast. We are called in this afterlife not just to a knowledge of God, but to total union with him as the lover, as the beloved.

Alleluia: For the Lord our God the Almighty reigns. Let us rejoice and exult and give him his glory, for the marriage of the Lamb has come, and his Bride has made herself ready; it was granted her to be clothed with fine linen, bright and pure. (Rev. 19:6–8)

While on earth, there will be moments of love when the Spirit calls me forth in the depths of my being to taste the Spirit in peace and to rest and abide in love. This is a prefiguration of the eternal wedding feast. It is the beginning of eternal life, to know and rest in the Father.

> And this is eternal life, that they know thee the only true God, and Jesus Christ whom thou hast sent. (John 17:3)

These fleeting moments of love which can certainly inspire and orient all our lives will flower out in totality when we meet the Father face to face. Kiss to kiss. There in the life to come, after our bodies have died and especially when they are risen, we will explode into the wedding feast, we will enter the eternal celebration.   — BNA, 132–33

It is up to each of us to discover how he or she is called to be more fully "clothed in Christ," in order for us to serve our brothers and sisters with love, kindness, and humility. It is up to each one to come closer to those who are "below," to help them stand up, to listen to them, to ask their advice, to meet them just as they are, with all their differences, to be one with them.

Jesus insists that the disciples wash each other's feet. He tells Peter that it is not optional but absolutely necessary to have his feet washed by Jesus, otherwise "you will have no part in me." Jesus affirms that, by doing this, he is giving us all an example to be followed, and that it is a beatitude, a blessing. All this is certainly because Jesus wants us to have an inner attitude of humility and service at all times. But he is also affirming the importance of actually washing each other's feet. This act of humility expresses in a very concrete way our love and respect for others.

Isn't this the logic of the sacraments? Each one signifies physically a gift of life and of love. The water of baptism cleanses us and gives us new life; the consecrated bread, broken, given and eaten, and the consecrated wine, offered and consumed, are all signs through which Jesus gives himself to us, so that we may

live continually in communion with him, in a heart-to-heart relationship. The sacraments are signs of the gift and at the same
time are real instruments of the gift, as long as we receive them
with faith, trust, and love; Jesus cannot give himself to us unless
we welcome him into our hearts.   —*SS*, 84–85

READING THE GOSPELS

August 1997
Orval Monastery

Dear Friends,

...This last year Jesus has led me more deeply into John's
Gospel. I always feel the need to be in direct contact with Scripture, the Word of God, the words of Jesus....It is as if John is
taking me by the hand and leading me into a deeper union with
Jesus in order to discover more totally his message of love. Let
me explain.

After the prologue, John's Gospel begins as John the Baptist
points to Jesus, calling him the "Lamb of God," not a powerful
leader or a strutting general or a politician seeking acclaim and
votes, but a lamb. This gentle lamb attracts two of John the
Baptist's disciples, Andrew and (most probably) John, who start
to follow him. Jesus turns to them and asks, "What are you
looking for?" They reply, "Where do you live?" They want to
be with him, to sit at his feet and learn from him. "Come and
see," says Jesus.

Then Jesus attracts or calls his first followers. Over a short
period of only two or three years, he forms and transforms their
hearts, their inner attitudes and motivations.

Do you know where he brings them first of all? To a wedding feast in Cana! Why? Because "the kingdom of God is like
a wedding feast." A wedding is a sign of love, unity, peace, fecundity, where a man and a woman become one flesh. We are
not all called to be married, but we are all called to the wedding
feast of the Lamb as described in the book of Revelation. The

celebration in Cana, however, is not an ordinary wedding. It is a celebration where water will be changed into wine. Our humanity is called to be transformed by God, our hearts of stone into hearts of flesh, so that the ecstasy of life, light, and love becomes ours.

Then Jesus reveals to his disciples that he is the new temple where God resides; his body is now the place of love, of forgiveness, of communion, from which all life and love flow. Then Nicodemus is shown to us, and with him Jesus reveals that the ultimate gift of ecstasy, of total fulfillment for each one of us, comes only as we are born anew, from above, transformed by water and the Spirit.

After that Jesus does not lead his followers to a school of learning but to people in pain. He reveals to them the compassion in his own heart toward the poor, the broken, the oppressed, and how he comes to bring them life and hope: a good news. He takes them first to a poor woman, of another religion and ethnic group, a woman of ill repute, who is alone and lonely and who feels guilty; she has lived already with five different men. Then they meet a poor father, crushed by pain; his little boy is dying. Then they go to the local psychiatric hospital or asylum, the pool of Bethesda, where "there were crowds of sick people: blind, lame, and paralyzed." I myself have visited many such places in our world; they are the places where all the unwanted are dumped. I am touched that this is one of the first places Jesus brings his disciples to, so that they may meet people who are broken, rejected, and in pain, and discover how he sees them, is close to them and loves them. Then the disciples begin to experience their own hearts opening up in compassion.

— *OLT*, 433–36

Peter's Denial of Jesus

Peter could not stand pain.

When Jesus was arrested and led away to a mock trial,

Peter said three times:
"I do not know that man!"
Matthew even tells us that the third time
Peter began to swear and to cry out:
"I do not know that man!"
Peter was not a man who was easily frightened.
He was courageous,
always ready to fight for the one he loved;
he was ready to die for Jesus.
He had told Jesus: "I will give my life for you,"
and yet later he says, "I do not know that man!"

Something has broken inside Peter and he starts to doubt.
Strangely enough, it is true: he does not know this man;
he does not recognize in this weak, battered person
the man who had spoken with authority,
the man who had performed miracles
and called Peter to follow him.
Peter had been attracted and seduced by a powerful Jesus.
He had followed Jesus because of his power....

Peter had witnessed the healings,
the multiplication of bread,
the transfiguration,
the resurrection of Lazarus,
and the fervor of the crowds.
He was fascinated by the freedom, and the strength
of Jesus' words;
the deep unity between what Jesus said and what he did;
by the newness of his message
and the way it brought life to others.

Peter believed that Jesus was the Messiah
who would liberate Israel from the occupying Roman army
and give a new dignity, freedom and power to his people.
Peter had a dream of a messianic triumph,
and it was becoming a reality.

He would be on the "winning team."
Too often, we dream of being on the winning team
whether it be in sports, in politics, in community,
or even in church.
…We all want to be part of a group
that is on the "right side" and that will triumph over others.

Faced with the weakness and littleness of Jesus,
Peter does not and cannot understand.
The Holy Spirit has not yet revealed to him
that Jesus gives life — gives life to all humankind —
not only by his words, his acts, and his miracles
but especially by the love of his heart,
which brought him to give his life in sacrifice.

We all have to make the same journey as Peter
and so come to a greater understanding
that those who are blessed
are not those who succeed "religiously"
but those who keep trusting
even as they live the experience of failure.
When we succeed in something, we naturally feel blessed.
But how can we feel blessed
when we are put aside, disregarded, humiliated?
How can we discover that failure is not merely negative?
Are we not scandalized by the extreme "failure" of life
which is death?
How can we understand
that the one who is dying on the cross,
in poverty and rejection,
— the one who keeps on trusting in spite of rejection —
is indeed blessed by God?   — BTS, 91–93

The Risen Jesus Appears to Mary Magdalene

There is something so humble in the story of the resurrection.
The risen Jesus does not appear triumphant over the Temple

to signify to everyone his victory
and to humiliate those who humiliated him.
He appears to Mary of Magdala,
the loved one, the forgiven one,
alone in a garden.
Jesus shares a simple, heart-to-heart relationship with her,
a gentle moment of eternity.
He does not appear with power but with a gentle love.
Calling Mary by her name,
he echoes the words of the prophet Isaiah:

> "Do not fear for I have redeemed [liberated] you.
> I have called you by name and you are mine....
> You are precious to my eyes and honored
> and I love you." (Isa. 43:1, 4)

Mary discovers a new relationship with Jesus.
She must not try to possess him and cling to him,
or seek to be the only one loved by him.
She must not hold on to the past
but live in the present moment
in a new, more interior relationship with the risen Jesus.
This relationship is a mutual indwelling,
he in her, and she in him,
and it will be given fully at Pentecost
with a new gift of the Spirit.

Jesus does not want her to cling to him.
He sends her forth to the community,
to those men with whom she must surely be angry,
who lacked compassion for her when she was upset.
Hadn't they abandoned Jesus at the cross?
Yet Jesus often sends us where we do not want to go!
How difficult it must be
to go from an intimate encounter with Jesus
to the larger community with all its needs and expectations!
Mary runs and announces to these men

that she has seen the Lord
and that he has called them his "brothers...."

Who is this woman who was all alone,
in the dark of the early hours of the day,
weeping and wailing,
frantically seeking the dead body of Jesus?
And why does the Evangelist devote so much time to her
and so little to the other disciples?

The answer takes us to the heart of the message of Jesus.
The Gospel of John shows how this woman
is an important sign
for all of us.

Mary does indeed represent each one of us.
Like her, we run here and there frantically,
each one of us alone, feeling empty,
wailing and weeping for a key to peace,
seeking a dead body,
a Jesus who lived some two thousand years ago.
Then Jesus, whom she seeks,
finds her and calls her by name.
So, too, each of us is waiting to be found
and called by our name.   —*DMJ*, 337–39

Epilogue

A Vision

Vanier's key question in the first selection is "Do we want to win or do we want to be in solidarity with others?" The second selection lays out how communities can change political structures, because structures are "the mirror of hearts." Peace is "not a question of stopping this or that catastrophe, but of rediscovering a vision," Vanier urges in selections from his 2003 book, Finding Peace. *A letter from 1994 calls readers "to believe that each gesture has its weight in the balance of love and hate in the world." Two unpublished letters written in 2008 conclude this section. At New Year, Vanier explores how apparent disasters can be turned into blessings. His May 2008 letter, written from Kenya, gently celebrates our unexpected life adventures as pilgrims and Vanier's own journey as he turns eighty.*

There is a beautiful story of a young man with a disability who wanted to win the Special Olympics; he got to the hundred meter race and he was running like crazy to get that gold medal. One of the others running with him slipped and fell; he turned round and picked him up and they ran across the finishing line together last. Are we prepared to sacrifice the prize for solidarity? It's a big question. Do we want to win or do we want to be in solidarity with others? Why is the gap between the rich and

the poor growing? Or the gap between the powerful and the
powerless? Between those who are the oppressors and the oppressed? We have to look at the poorest and the weakest. They
have a message to give us. Living with these people — different,
fragile, vulnerable, anguished people — has revealed what is the
most beautiful in me, but also what is the most terrible. I have
discovered that the anguish of some people with disabilities has
awoken my anguish.

We need transformation because there is so much tension and
egoism in us. We see the world only through our own eyes;
we are not liberated to see people as God sees them. We see
people through our wounds, through our difficulties, through
our prejudices. We need to be liberated to see people with disabilities as God sees them. To see people of other cultures as
God sees them. To be liberated in the way we look at them and
seek to understand them. We all have fears and prejudices. It is
important to discover where our anger and violence came from
and how to live with them. It is important to find a way of
transformation so that fear and hate can be transformed into
positive energies. It's a long road. The water has to be changed
into wine. The whole of the vision of Jesus, which is the vision of peace, is about coming out from behind barriers and
discovering people as they are.   — EO, 18–19

Some Christians are very taken up by politics. They can be terribly anti-communist, forming rather fascist organizations to
fight the "red devil." Or they can be fiercely anti-capitalist,
fighting for new structures and redistribution of resources.
Both these tendencies can lead to a centralization — whether
to protect the free-market economy or to further wholesale
nationalization.

I sometimes wonder if these fighting Christians wouldn't do
better to put their energies into creating communities which
live as far as they can by the charter of the Beatitudes. If they
did this, they would be able to live by, and measure progress
by, values other than those of material success, acquisition of

wealth, and political struggle. They could become the yeast in the dough of society. They would not change political structures at first. But they would change the hearts and spirits of the people around them by offering them a glimpse of a new dimension in human life—that of inwardness, love, contemplation, wonderment, and sharing. They would introduce people to a place where the weak and poor, far from being pushed aside, are central to their society. My personal hope is that, if this spirit of community really spreads, structures will change. Structures are — tyrannies excepted — the mirrors of hearts. But if change is to come, some people should be working now on the political level toward a society which is more just, true, and sharing, in which communities can take root and shine, and where human beings can be truly human.

Something similar could be said about people who throw themselves militantly into causes. Some people struggling for peace are terribly aggressive, even with "rival" peace movements. To struggle for a cause it is best for people to be rooted in a community where they are learning reconciliation, acceptance of difference and of their own darkness, and how to celebrate. Isn't there a danger when groups with noble humanitarian causes develop very aggressive attitudes and divide the world into "goodies" and "baddies"? This type of elitism can be dangerous and continues a form of apartheid and oppression toward those who do not share the same ideas.   —CG, 308–9

The events of September 11 called me to become personally committed to peacemaking, to continue to reflect on peace and on the sources of violence in our world, in me, and in each one of us.

People from various cultures and religions as well as people with no specific religious tradition came together after the attacks to pray and to affirm together their vision of mutual acceptance and their esteem and love for all human beings. And yet the evenings of prayer I participated in left me a bit uneasy. I felt as though people were not praying for a new just order between people and nations, but, motivated by fear, were pray-ing to keep the status quo — no change, no insecurity, nothing that would disturb their lives or views on the world....

My hope is that more and more people will discover that the peace we all yearn for is not just the work of governments but the task of each one of us. We can all become makers of peace. We can do our part. The future of the world is in the hands of each of us, and it depends on our commitment to-gether with others for peace, each according to our own gifts and responsibilities. Peace is not a question of stopping this or that catastrophe, but of rediscovering a vision, a path of hope for all of humanity.   — *FP*, 4–6

Since September 11, 2001, many are also hiding behind preju-dice and fear, stigmatizing those of other cultures. And perhaps in our times the darkness will grow darker, more towers and certitudes will crumble, and stock exchanges will wobble again before more of us truly begin to search for new ways of living, new ways of peace.

The world will not, of course, change overnight. But the gravity of our times, the fear of war, terrorism, and all forms of violence are inciting many men and women to search for a new way of life. Many have seen through the shallowness of mate-rial prosperity and are discovering that they can be an active part of peacemaking.

If you and I seek today to live peace, to be peacemakers, to help create communities of peace, it is not just to seek success. If we find peace, live and work for peace, even if we see no tangible results, we can become fully human beings, walking together on the road of kindness, compassion, and peace. New hope is born.   — *FP*, 82

World events, particularly in Haiti, Bosnia, and Rwanda, make me feel confused: our societies continue to live superficial val-ues as if nothing was happening, as if it were too difficult, even impossible, to look at the truth of our world.

Each one of us must continue to trust that we can do something to stop the indifference, fear, and evil. Wherever we are, we can pray and keep our hearts open and loving; we can struggle against lies and hatred in us and around us. We can be close to those around us who are in pain; we can work each day to create communities that are warm and open, founded on the love of God. It would be awful if the terrible suffering of our world paralyzed and blinded us in regard to the pain of those who are close by.

There are also many many gestures of love and support given in Rwanda, people who have given their lives to save others. The heart of God rejoices in all the gestures of love, of sharing, and of sacrifice in the midst of all the suffering. Each one of us is called to believe that our small acts of love and hope can help our brothers and sisters in Rwanda, Bosnia, and Haiti, that each gesture has its weight in the balance of love and hate in our world. Wherever we are, we can enter more fully into the struggle and the offering of love.

—Letter, August 1994, *OLT*, 411–12

New Year 2008

Dear friends,

At a retreat that I gave in Lithuania last October for Faith and Light groups and people who wanted to start L'Arche, there was a mother who shared very movingly about her life.

When her daughter was born with a disability she saw it as a curse. Whenever she used public transport and people would look at her and her daughter with curiosity and sometimes malevolence, she at times felt that she didn't want to live anymore. Then one day she went into a church where she saw a group of people, some of whom had disabilities, who were happy, laughing, and dancing. It was a Faith and Light community. Afterward she joined Faith and Light and what she had seen as a curse became a blessing.

For many parents their child's disability can appear to be a disaster. For many people in our world life can appear to be a disaster. What does it take for a disaster to become a blessing? Isn't this the question that we can all ask ourselves? How can we help to build communities that can become a source of blessing for those who feel they are living a disaster?

We hear more and more about the disasters that risk affecting our earth: environmental and climatic, terrorism and wars. Apparently, these risks are increasing with the industrial development of China and India and many other countries that want to make up for lost time as regards their economy.... There is a sort of mad race for development which risks taking humanity toward the greatest crisis it has ever known. Is this a disaster?

Hélène Elsida, a professor of economy and theology, said in a recent public conference that this crisis could be a great opportunity for humanity! This disaster could become a blessing. ...Together, not through competition or struggle, but through joint dialogue and research, we will find solutions, peaceful solutions.

And these solutions will imply less speed and mobility and more interiority: less consumption and more relationships; less technology and more humanity; less dissipation and more unity; less competitiveness and more community; less individualism and more sharing and living together.

It is Christmas time: a new year is beginning. It is a time when we want to live peace. We celebrate the birth of a child, the birth of the Child.... We must listen to this child who is filled with wonder and who contemplates, who teaches us to play, to laugh, to celebrate, to dance, to relax, to love one another, to exchange gifts, to embrace one another.... Let us build together a world of children, for children, where there is less competition and more celebration and dance....

God is so vulnerable, so loving, so humble in the face of our freedom. And God is ever new. God makes all things new. Happy Christmas, Happy New Year. May this year be a blessed year for all of us.

Pray for me that I may continue on the path that Jesus gives me to take.
                                                            Jean Vanier

May 2008

Dear friends,

Here I am in Kenya. You may well ask, "Why has my pilgrimage brought me to this African country which went through a lot of turmoil recently?" Well, it's a long story!...

I am a pilgrim. We are all pilgrims. My life has been a pilgrimage. Soon I will be going though the gate of my eightieth birthday. I feel excited. What is that gate opening up for me? A new life?

I hope and pray that when the moment of greater weakness comes for me that I can laugh and rejoice and be happy with what will be given to me....

It is a gentle time for me as I come to the end of this period of my life, where in the future I will travel less, and no more visit communities. I had dreamt of going to Vietnam and China, I had dreamt of returning to the Ivory Coast to visit our community and see and share again with N'Goran and others. I had dreamt of returning to Haiti, and to our communities in Latin America....

My dream now is to live in my community, in my home, to live a simple life in Trosly. I will try to live what I have preached for so many years, hoping to be a support and not a burden to my community, trying to deepen my relationship with Jesus and with my brothers and sisters. I will continue, as long as I can, to give retreats at the Farm, the little spiritual center at the heart of L'Arche. My joy is to announce Jesus and the love of God, to announce the presence of God in those who are the most vulnerable and to announce also the humility and the vulnerability of God.

So I am a pilgrim wanting to live well the last stage of my life not as a loss of activities but of gaining a new way to live. I am also realizing how L'Arche and all our communities are like pilgrims. Pilgrims are heading for a holy place, and their hearts want to be holy. The pilgrimage is filled with the unexpected: surprise meetings with beautiful people, accidents, sore feet and blisters, horrible weather (raining or too hot), and all the rest.

There is no real security except pilgrims know where they are going: the holy place....

For some of you it will soon be holiday time (for others it will soon be winter). Holiday time is holy days. I will be in my monastery in Belgium. Time to rest, to pray, to read, to walk, to listen to the birds, to listen to the gentle music of God. I will be in communion with you — be it holy days or winter days (days of stress . . .), let us pray for each other and for all in our world who are suffering from loneliness and despair.

Peace, peace, peace.

Jean Vanier

Permissions

The publisher gratefully acknowledges permission from the following publishers for permission to reprint material by Jean Vanier:

House of Anansi for excerpts from *Becoming Human*, copyright © 1998 by Jean Vanier and the Canadian Broadcasting Corporation; *Made for Happiness: Discovering the Meaning of Life with Aristotle*, © 2001 by Jean Vanier; *Finding Peace*, © 2003 by Jean Vanier. Reprinted with permission from House of Anansi Press, Toronto.

William B. Eerdmans Publishing Company, Grand Rapids, Michigan, for excerpts from Jean Vanier, *Befriending the Stranger*, © 2005. Reprinted by permission of the publisher; all U.S. rights reserved.

Continuum International Publishing Group (London) for excerpts from *Finding Peace*, © 2006. By kind permission of Continuum.

Paulist Press for excerpts from *Becoming Human* by Jean Vanier © 1999 by Jean Vanier and the Canadian Broadcasting Corporation; *Community and Growth* by Jean Vanier. Translation © 1979 by Jean Vanier, 2nd rev. ed., © 1989 by Jean Vanier; *Encountering the Other* by Jean Vanier, © 2005; *Drawn into the Mystery of Jesus through the Gospel of John* by Jean Vanier, © 2004; *Man and Woman God Made Them*, © 1984 by Editions Fleurus, Paris, © 1984 by Editions Bellarmin, Montreal, English translation © 1985, 2008; *From Brokenness to Community*, © 1992; *Seeing Beyond Depression*